IFLA Publications

Edited by
Michael Heaney

International Federation of Library Associations and Institutions
Fédération Internationale des Associations de Bibliothécaires et des Bibliothèques
Internationaler Verband der bibliothekarischen Vereine und Institutionen
Международная Федерация Библиотечных Ассоциаций и Учреждений
Federación Internacional de Asociaciones de Bibliotecarios y Bibliotecas
国际图书馆协会与机构联合会
الاتحاد الدولي لجمعيات ومؤسسات المكتبات

Volume 162

IFLA

Linked Data and User Interaction

The Road Ahead

Edited on behalf of IFLA by
H. Frank Cervone and Lars G. Svensson

DE GRUYTER
SAUR

ISBN 978-3-11-031692-6
e-ISBN (PDF) 978-3-11-031700-8
e-ISBN (EPUB) 978-3-11-039616-4
ISSN 0344-6891

Library of Congress Cataloging-in-Publication Data
A CIP catalog record for this book has been applied for at the Library of Congress.

Bibliografische Information der Deutschen Nationalbibliothek
The Deutsche Nationalbibliothek lists this publication in the Deutsche Nationalbibliografie; detailed bibliographic data is available on the internet at http://dnb.dnb.de.

Cover Image: Directed network diagram of linked data elements (c) 2015 H. Frank Cervone
Typesetting: Dr Rainer Ostermann, München
Printing and binding: CPI books GmbH, Leck
♾ Printed on acid-free paper
Printed in Germany

www.degruyter.com

Contents

About IFLA — VII

H. Frank Cervone
Linked Data and User Interaction: An Introduction — 1

Paola Di Maio
1 **Linked Data Beyond Libraries**
Towards Universal Interfaces and Knowledge Unification — **3**

Emmanuelle Bermès
2 **Following the User's Flow in the Digital Pompidou — 19**

Patrick Le Bœuf
3 **Customized OPACs on the Semantic Web**
The OpenCat Prototype — **31**

Ryan Shaw, Patrick Golden and Michael Buckland
4 **Using Linked Library Data in Working Research Notes — 48**

Timm Heuss, Bernhard Humm, Tilman Deuschel, Torsten Fröhlich, Thomas Herth and Oliver Mitesser
5 **Semantically Guided, Situation-Aware Literature Research — 66**

Niklas Lindström and Martin Malmsten
6 **Building Interfaces on a Networked Graph — 85**

Natasha Simons, Arve Solland and Jan Hettenhausen
7 **Griffith Research Hub**
Connecting an Entire University's Research Enterprise — **98**

Contributors — 119

Index — 120

About IFLA

www.ifla.org

IFLA (The International Federation of Library Associations and Institutions) is the leading international body representing the interests of library and information services and their users. It is the global voice of the library and information profession. IFLA provides information specialists throughout the world with a forum for exchanging ideas and promoting international cooperation, research, and development in all fields of library activity and information service. IFLA is one of the means through which libraries, information centres, and information professionals worldwide can formulate their goals, exert their influence as a group, protect their interests, and find solutions to global problems.

IFLA's aims, objectives, and professional programme can only be fulfilled with the co-operation and active involvement of its members and affiliates. Currently, approximately 1,600 associations, institutions and individuals, from widely divergent cultural backgrounds, are working together to further the goals of the Federation and to promote librarianship on a global level. Through its formal membership, IFLA directly or indirectly represents some 500,000 library and information professionals worldwide.

IFLA pursues its aims through a variety of channels, including the publication of a major journal, as well as guidelines, reports and monographs on a wide range of topics. IFLA organizes workshops and seminars around the world to enhance professional practice and increase awareness of the growing importance of libraries in the digital age. All this is done in collaboration with a number of other non-governmental organizations, funding bodies and international agencies such as UNESCO and WIPO. IFLANET, the Federation's website, is a prime source of information about IFLA, its policies and activities: www.ifla.org.

Library and information professionals gather annually at the IFLA World Library and Information Congress, held in August each year in cities around the world.

IFLA was founded in Edinburgh, Scotland, in 1927 at an international conference of national library directors. IFLA was registered in the Netherlands in 1971. The Koninklijke Bibliotheek (Royal Library), the national library of the Netherlands, in The Hague, generously provides the facilities for our headquarters. Regional offices are located in Rio de Janeiro, Brazil; Pretoria, South Africa; and Singapore.

Linked Data and User Interaction: An Introduction

The book that is in your hands is the culmination of several years' work by some of the best and brightest minds in the information sciences. The topic of user interaction based on library linked data had its origin in a satellite meeting of the 2013 International Federation of Library Associations' (IFLA) World Library and Information Congress (WLIC). The volume you are reading is an edited version of the majority of the talks and presentations at that satellite meeting held in Singapore.

As was noted in the original call for papers, the amount of linked data that is being made available through libraries and other information agencies has increased dramatically in the last several years. Following the lead of the National Library of Sweden in 2008, several libraries and library networks have begun to publish authority files and bibliographic information as open, linked data. While providing data is an important step in making information more accessible to a wide audience, applications that consume this data are also a critical component in the information ecosphere. Today, the use of linked data is not yet widespread. In particular, a specific problem is that there are no widely used methods for integrating linked data from multiple sources or significant agreement on how this data should be presented in end user interfaces. Existing services tend to build on one or two well integrated datasets – often from the same data supplier – and do not actively use the links provided to other datasets within or outside of the library or cultural heritage sector to provide a better user experience.

The main objective of the satellite meeting was to provide a forum for discussion of services, concepts, and approaches that focus on the interaction between the end user and linked data from libraries and other cultural heritage institutions. Of particular interest were papers presenting working end user interfaces using linked data from both cultural heritage institutions (including libraries) and other datasets.

Special thanks must be extended to several people who were active members in the IFLA Information Technology Standing Committee (ITSC) at the time:

- Alenka Kavčič-Čolić, then chair of the ITSC;
- Reinhard Altenhöner, past chair of the ITSC;
- Edmund Balnaves, current chair of the ITSC;
- Lars G. Svensson, current secretary of the ITSC; and

- Emmanuelle Bermès, chair of the semantic web special interest group who actively pursued making the satellite meeting a reality.

H. Frank Cervone
Chicago, IL
Past secretary of the IFLA Information Technology Section
IT Standing Committee member, 2007–2015

Paola Di Maio

1 Linked Data Beyond Libraries

Towards Universal Interfaces and Knowledge Unification

Introduction

There have been many talks about linked data. Writing up a keynote address on the topic is a privilege, given the illustrious speakers who have preceded me, yet it can be a hard act to follow. I consider it a great opportunity to stand on the shoulders of giants and look forward and will try to expand the vision further.

From the technical to the socio-technical

From a technical point of view, linked data has been discussed at great length. It is proposed as a mechanism to tackle challenges such as information overload, mostly from a computational perspective, where the priority concerns tend to be increasing the efficiency of the computational performance, the handling of large datasets, scalability. The focus has been mostly about quantitative issues such as how to publish and query zillion triples type of challenges, and how to increase quality, such as precision and recall, of search results from large datasets.

This talk contributes a socio-technical systems perspective to linked data discourse. For most purposes, we can define socio-technical systems as being made up of people, technologies and the environment. The latter is intended not only as a physical, geographical environment made of water and air, but also the cultural environment, made up of heterogeneous social norms and wide-ranging cognitive patterns. This perspective considers the web as a "Digital Ecosystem", essentially an open, unbounded, partially ordered (chaotic even) digital space, which accounts for the existence of multiple dimensions and multiple goals, often appearing to be conflicting.

Complexity and Multidimensionality

There is no single matrix to define complexity exhaustively. For example the complexity of natural systems can be defined by the density of interactions of a system's components, functions and processes, among other factors and by the regularity and predictability of their dynamics and patterns.

In social systems complexity is characterized by innumerable additional dimensions corresponding to the diversity and richness of human traits, from the cognitive to the behavioural, the ethical and emotional, from the individual to the collective, to name just a few.

As a pertinent example, at least two views of linked data models are commonly promoted (Figure 1.1). Such a dichotomy is possibly the result of different points of view, which can be very resource intensive, and at times even pointless, to resolve. Either way our knowledge is partial/incomplete/imperfect, with very few exceptions. Language, logic and the unrefined cognitive apparatus are not perfect, with very few exceptions, and can prompt a view of the world full of contradictions and paradoxes.

Figure 1.1: Two views of linked data.

Alignment

In a world full of apparent contradictions and paradoxes, where systems are multi-dimensional and support a multiplicity of goals, it can help to shift the perspective to achieve some alignment of the dimensions which make it up. It may be a good idea to create layered systems that can achieve multiple goals simultaneously.

Dichotomies aside, linked data common sense is getting a hold in the information technology community. And linked library data has a lively user base of early adopters, as a glue to bridge across the babel of existing library data standards such as FRBR (Functional Requirements for Bibliographic Records) and RDA (Resource Description and Access).[1]

The *Report of the Stanford Linked Data Workshop*[2] provides some useful definitions:

> "Library data" is any type of digital information produced or curated by libraries that describes resources or aids their discovery. Data covered by library privacy policies is generally out of scope. This report pragmatically distinguishes three types of library data based on their typical use: datasets, element sets, and value vocabularies.
>
> "Linked data" refers to data published in accordance with principles designed to facilitate linkages among datasets, element sets, and value vocabularies.

A report published by the W3C LLD Incubator Group[3] informs us that:

> ... Although the level of maturity or stability of available resources varies greatly – many existing resources are the result of ongoing project work or the result of individual initiatives, and describe themselves as prototypes rather than mature offerings – the abundance of such efforts is a sign of activity around and interest in library linked data, exemplifying the processes of rapid prototyping and "agile" development that linked data supports. At the same time, the need for such creative, dynamically evolving efforts is counterbalanced by a need for library linked data resources that are stable and available for the long term.... Established institutions are increasingly committing resources to linked data projects, from the national libraries of Sweden, Hungary, Germany, France, the Library of Congress, and the British Library, to the Food and Agriculture Organization of the United Nations and OCLC Online Computer Library Center, Inc. Such institutions provide a stable foundation on which library linked data can grow over time.

In the case of underlying well-formed information structures, such as data which has been exported from relational databases or integrated library systems, linked data works well and this may be the case for the majority of linked library data, and possibly one of the reasons of its relative success.

1 http://www.slideshare.net/rjw/library-linked-data-progress. Accessed on 17 December 2014.

2 http://www.clir.org/pubs/reports/pub152/LinkedDataWorkshop.pdf. Accessed on 17 December 2014.

3 http://www.w3.org/2005/Incubator/lld/XGR-lld-20111025/. Accessed on 17 December 2014.

Limitations and challenges encountered are mostly due to fragmentation, heterogeneity, as we learn from related communities of practice,[4] these are very common issues in human cognition and knowledge organization.

I like to think of linked data as part of a greater whole, whereby the greater whole is the universe of discourse on the web, and linked data is one way, possibly the simplest way worked out so far if modelled and implemented correctly, to represent and leverage some basic degree of semantics, where semantics is intended as bearing meaning (Maienborn, von Heusinger and Portner 2011). Thinking holistically is very much part of a systemic view of the world, and it really helps to get to grips with the incommensurability of the real world.

Despite the relative success of the linked data meme, unresolved semantic web practical issues and challenges haven't gone away. Those who have been around a while may have seen them discussed more or less productively for ages. There are many open issues in relation to categorization, conceptualization, capturing and representing paradigms and worldviews, communication.

For me, taking linked data beyond libraries means taking the vision and the good practices and lessons learned beyond the virtual wall of a well understood domain. Library data benefits, generally speaking, from a great degree of granularity and structure. Thanks to centuries of library science, and the dedication of meticulous, admittedly sometimes even obsessive and pedantic librarians and curators, library datasets are among the most refined and finely shaped, capable of facing information retrieval challenges of various sorts, which are increasing due to the information explosion. Users face the challenges of information retrieval, once associated mostly with libraries, everyday across the open web.

In the last twenty years, since the web started transforming the world into an open network of nodes the majority of which are publishing something online, real-time information retrieval on the web has become a nightmare. Thanks only to powerful technologies such as indexing, crawlers and search algorithms, it is possible to leverage the wealth of online data, although quite a lot of manual sorting and knowledge intensive parsing are required to gather actual intelligence from typical search results

Linked Library data can serve as a mirror of how linked data could work in other domains too, because it is arguably where data is shaped at its best, and because Library data is the perfect model for "world knowledge". Libraries have historically been the sole repositories of artefacts of explicit knowledge. So linked library data can be a model of what works, and how, possibly supplying a cradle of test cases and good practices.

---

4 http://www.slideshare.net/DanielVilaSuero/status-quo-and-current-limitations-of-library-linked-data. Accessed on 17 December 2014.

Information fragmentation, heterogeneity and duplication are challenges in all fields of human knowledge. Linked or not, library data should not be another island! We should not think of library data versus non-library data, because that would not make sense, in a way it would be defeating the purpose of linking, if we separate library from non-library data.

In the open web, nobody benefits from data islands. Digital ecosystems come with risks and fragility: for example, wrong false or incorrect data can be propagated virally through a network of systems, irreversibly. But a healthy ecosystem should not propagate blindly, it can be designed to be self-correcting via fact checking and cross referencing. (But this is for another talk, perhaps.)

Conceptual islands are also not nice. Linking data can take place pragmatically, by exposing and connecting data structures, but inevitably it must be first addressed at conceptual level. It's not just a mechanical thing of syntax. When concept A relates to concept B, even in the relatively simplified linked data world, some implications must be considered.

If it's true that everything is related to everything else in some way, then linked data can help discover these relations, yet while trying to ensure minimal constraint for creative thinking, some ontological duty of attempting to model reality correctly remains.

If we think of library linked data as an open model of all knowledge that exists, then in principle it can be considered a generic schema which can serve as gateway to universal knowledge. Although some may argue that no such thing exists, I consider it the only possible way to escape from the cognitive cage.

By cognitive cage I mean whatever constrains the mind (which is possibly also what prevents it from wandering off). It could be partial/incomplete knowledge, it could be worldview, assumptions, beliefs or any kind of ontological artificial safeguard. But also any fixed ontological view, held axioms, categories and rules and logic behind them. While these can help constrain cognition to the purpose of supporting basic intelligent functions, they can also probably create an arbitrary partition of what is true.

In fact, ontologies, taxonomies and categories can be helpful in forming a logical structure to support human cognition such as learning and knowing about the world, however on the other hand, they are often arbitrarily constructed based on a given worldview, which typically conforms to an existing scientific paradigm, potentially and paradoxically inhibiting the shift to a new paradigm. This could inhibit alternative cognitive trajectories and the discovery of new inference paths, which could possibly lead to alternate conclusions or to a much more integrated view.

Human cognition, and everything that rests upon it, is built around categories and logical relations, and makes ample use of all the devices and artefacts which have evolved in the course of the modern history of logic and philosophy. but it is important in my view to realize that these are instruments which allow humans to comprehend, make sense of, represent and communicate reality, however they are not reality itself, which in its complexity and incommensurability, is "beyond cognition". Yet human behaviour is directly determined, defined and triggered by the knowledge that humans hold. Optimal behaviour – whether operational or social – depends on the availability of optimal knowledge.

Set knowledge categories and compartmentalized information structures inhibit creative behaviours and potentially inhibit genius. In a related contribution,[5] I refer to the dissolution of artificial conceptual boundaries into a kind of direct experiential enlightenment as cognitive climax, a step towards deeper cognitive insights, perhaps. Today, thanks to web based technologies and approaches such as linked data, knowledge discovery has the potential not only to support information retrieval and knowledge discovery at exponential rate, but also to explore creative reasoning for example. Yet there is no science as of today capable of dynamic knowledge discovery that supports ontological emergence, which is not what exists, but what **is becoming**.

Linked library data, and linked data in general, perhaps, could support ontological emergence, and although some of the challenges in the information age are purely cognitive – technical, socio-technical and philosophical issues aside – linked data can help to tackle them.

From "Knowledge Discovery" towards Unification

Although not realistically quantifiable, incommensurable amounts of explicitly represented knowledge exists, collected, sorted and ordered in libraries. Hard to imagine that what is known, however incommensurable, is only a small fragment of the knowledge yet to be discovered and acquired, assuming that humanity will continue to learn.

Not all knowledge that exists is documented, recorded, nor scientifically validated – much has been lost throughout history and is lost or hidden from the public view. Thanks to the web whatever knowledge is publicly available is becoming increasingly accessible, hence potentially "usable", yet many new challenges arise:

- distilling very big open data sets which are becoming available (thanks also to open access guerrilla movements) into meaningful, usable and useful

5 http://www.slideshare.net/PaolaDIM/sw10-yearslides. Accessed on 17 December 2014.

general knowledge – so that existing knowledge can become widespread common sense and wisdom in decision-making;
- integrating knowledge from different domains into "higher-level knowledge" possibly resulting into a general intelligence;
- actually making the most of existing knowledge.

Even when knowledge is accessible, there is no way of telling whether it is used to inform decisions, and looking at contemporary politics one wonders how, despite the unprecedented availability of knowledge, why there is still so much nonsense – poor, unaccountable decision-making going on all around us?

Knowledge fragmentation describes the disconnectedness of different sets of knowledge, which can be due to different causes. This was the topic of the ASIST Award of Merit Acceptance Speech by Don R. Swanson "On the Fragmentation of Knowledge, the Connection Explosion, and Assembling Other People's Ideas" (Swanson 2001). I report some excerpts of Don's speech below, as they characterize the problem space with some clarity:

> Three aspects of the context and nature of this fragmentation seem notable:
>
> One, the disparity between the total quantity of recorded knowledge, however it might be measured, and the limited human capacity to assimilate it, is not only enormous now but grows unremittingly. Exactly how the limitations of the human intellect and life span affect the growth of knowledge is unknown.
>
> Two, in response to the information explosion, specialties are somehow spontaneously created, then grow too large and split further into subspecialties without even a declaration of independence. One unintended result is the fragmentation of knowledge owing to inadequate cross-specialty communication. And as knowledge continues to grow, fragmentation will inevitably get worse because it is driven by the human imperative to escape inundation.
>
> Three, of particular interest to me is the possibility that information in one specialty might be of value in another without anyone becoming aware of the fact. Specialized literatures, or other "units" of knowledge, that do not intercommunicate by citing one another may nonetheless have many implicit textual interconnections based on meaning. Indeed the number of unintended or implicit text-based connections within the literature of science may greatly exceed the number that are explicit, because there are far more possible combinations of units (that potentially could be related) than there are units. The connection explosion may be more portentous than the information explosion.

In his speech, Swanson recounts how he encountered, partly by accident, two pieces of information from two different articles in the medical literature that together suggested an answer to a question for which he could find no single article that provided an answer:

> It seemed that I might have found out something that no one else knew and that the medical literature might be full of such undiscovered connections. ... Most of my efforts since then have been directed toward developing a computer-assisted literature-based approach to scientific discovery... The purpose of the computer here is to organize and display information in a way that helps the user see new connections of scientific interest.

The need of a more coherent view of humanity's intellectual patrimony is expressed repeated by various authors:

> "In an increasingly complex world, the fragmented state of knowledge can be seen as one of the most pressing social problems of our time" and "History seems to attest that the absence of a collective worldview ostensibly condemns humanity to an endless series of conflicts that inevitably stem from incompatible, partially correct, locally situated justification systems." Good reasons for believing that if there was a shared, general background of explanation, humanity might be able to achieve much greater levels of harmonious relations (Henriques 2003).
>
> In this time of divisive tendencies within and between the nations, races, religions, sciences and humanities, synthesis must become the great magnet which orients us all...[Yet] scientists have not done what is possible toward integrating bodies of knowledge created by science into a unified interpretation of man, his place in nature, and his potentialities for creating the good society. Instead, they are entombing us in dark and meaningless catacombs of learning. (Reiser, cited in Henriques 2003)

Knowledge unification theories have been proposed by our contemporaries including E.O. Wilson, a biologist/entomologist who worked at Harvard, and various scientists and researchers working towards a general systems theory or a "Theory of Everything" (Wilson 2001, Bertalanffy 1972).

Linked data is the nearest publicly available artefact ever to make knowledge unification a *de facto* reality, which has the potential to overcome the inherent limitations of the first generation of web standards, concerned mostly with standardizing syntax on the web.

What is it about?

Taking linked library data as a good working example to show the benefits of linked data, if properly modelled and implemented, it looks fairly simple. It is about

- linking;
- data, knowledge, intelligence;
- interfaces.

Linking is a basic function of human cognition. We learn by making logical connections between what we know and what we discover. We reason by means of relations and correlations and by making more or less logical inferences.

In computer science, a linker or link editor is a computer program that takes one or more object files generated by a compiler and combines them into a single executable program.[6]

The fact that linking is an essential feature of the World Wide Web architecture is surely no coincidence. Talking about the global brain, the web (at its best) is clearly a living infrastructure which reflects and projects human knowledge in support of individual and collective cognition.

Although the meme under discussion is linked data, I'd like to take a moment to note how data is only the substrate of a much more complex piece of a knowledge model, whereby data is the most quantifiable chunk of information, upon which, however, layers of information and knowledge which support intelligent functions are built. Linked information and linked knowledge are also interesting and should be studied in more detail, maybe as an evolution of linked data.

Linked data Interfaces

Finally, we get to talk about interfaces, which is actually the rather important subject of this workshop and the focal point of this talk.

Interface design is an important discipline in human-computer interaction, and the subject of much study and discussion. Classical techniques to interface design are task decomposition, to help understand what task users should accomplish via the interface, and cognitive task analysis, to help designers understand what knowledge the user requires to perform these tasks, so that the interface can be designed accordingly to provide maximum support for the user. It should be noted that are many kinds of interfaces, which are not mutually exclusive. For example:

- graphic, text, sound;
- command line interfaces;
- touch user interface;
- attentive user interfaces which manage the user attention;
- batch interfaces i.e. non-interactive user interfaces;
- conversational interface agents;
- gesture interfaces;
- multi-screen interfaces.

6 http://en.wikipedia.org/wiki/Linker_(computing). Accessed on 17 December 2014.

Devising some knowledge representation for different kinds of interfaces could be flagged as work ahead.

When I first started talking to people about the need for easy to use interfaces for the semantic web, I was asked "In what way is a semantic web interface different from any other interface?"

For a start, new semantic capabilities offered by social web technologies are driven by new kinds of "tasks" and functions not generally available with other kinds of software, such as semantic search or semantic aggregation or queries spread across different datasets. Learning how to model these tasks hierarchically and cognitively should take us closer to where we want to be. I take inspiration from an extensive list of semantic capabilities described in a report by Project 10X (Davis) reproduced as a list in the Appendix.

Each "semantic capability" can be considered, from the user viewpoint, as a task. For example, a semantic search can be seen as the result of a different type of function than non-semantic search. The queried dataset, the relations, the visual layout of the outcome of a search carried out across multiple datasets and multiple sources, are different variables not always present in non-semantic search. This means that the user task of carrying out a semantic search is technically and functionally different from other searches, and as such it would be simplified and facilitated with an appropriate user interface, designed to isolate the end user from the complexity of a highly specialized technical function. Equally, lower-level interfaces for technical users can also be provided. The same applies for each semantic capability, which in tasks analysis correspond to a different task.

Where is it all going?

The challenges of knowledge integration/unification may require further paradigm shift for interfaces. From linked library data we can learn what works, and best practices. But we still need to think – sooner rather than later – of what kind of novel interfaces may be required to make the most of the powerful capabilities provided by new semantic technologies. I used to dream of universal interfaces to navigate linked data, dashboard-like front ends for the semantic web, not too dissimilar from what search engines already offer, a slot which given any input will provide a best answer based on a standard algorithm, with the possibility to change some values and parameters to define the context more precisely and obtain more customized answers. Nowadays we are starting to see such artefacts becoming available, and I and my peers can claim some of the merits for requesting to the semantic web such high-level features.

The notion of universal interfaces is well understood in engineering design, and it has been proposed before (Baxley 2003; Sturgeon 2001) although not in relation to linked data. In working towards Universal Interfaces for Knowledge Unification using a linked data approach, we are not just wishful thinkers. Science has recently started to observe and record systematically the notion of universality, which we must understand to help us guide the development of useful universal interfaces.

For example "Despite the complexity and diversity of nature, there exists universality in the form of critical scaling laws among various dissimilar systems and processes such as stock markets, earthquakes, crackling noise, lung inflation and vortices in superconductors. This universality is mainly independent of the microscopic details, depending only on the symmetry and dimension of the system. Exploring how universality is affected by the system dimensions is an important unresolved problem. Here we demonstrate experimentally that universality persists even at a dimensionality crossover in ferromagnetic nanowires" (Kim et al. 2009, 740).

Could linked-data experiments help us identify universality?

When we think of the need for novel approaches capable of leading towards knowledge unification, we need to study universality as it emerges from fragmentation, as described above, and how to bridge it.

Thankfully, principles of Universal Design have already been laid down, in relation to architecture for example: "designing all products ... to be aesthetic and usable to the greatest extent possible by everyone, regardless of age, ability, or status in life" (Center for Universal Design 2008).

Principles of Universal Design
1. Equitable use
2. Flexibility in use
3. Simple and intuitive
4. Perceptible information
5. Tolerance for error
6. Low effort

(Center for Universal Design 2008)

Linked-data interfaces should also support cross-referencing of different datasets in diverse fields of knowledge, and possibly facilitate creative reasoning.

In creating interfaces to guide users to traverse infinite possible knowledge configurations via linked datasets, it could be useful to keep in mind the principles of universal design. Sceptics may say that one size cannot fit all, but it depends how clever an artefact is.

Two textbook examples of universality in design are the award-winning Swiss knife and the universal plug adaptor, which can serve as useful metaphors to help linked data interface designers.

Conclusion and work ahead

To sum up, knowledge and experience from library linked data offer good practices and use cases that can be transferred to other domains. There will always be open challenges which can be addressed by taking a socio-technical/whole-systems approach; we must think big, and above all think "whole". The mission includes addressing paradoxes, harmonization, and knowledge/science unification by extending the technical system boundary to include people and their physical and cultural environments. I am confident that provided the data/information models are not inherently broken (as it is often the case mostly due to going straight into coding without proper analysis and design), many challenges in libraries and elsewhere can be addressed by linked data approaches, adequately supported by universal interfaces.

Appendix: Semantic Technologies Capabilities[7]

Answer Engine: To provide a direct reply to a search questions as opposed to returning a list of relevant documents. It interprets a question asked in a natural language, checks multiple data sources to collect knowledge nuggets required for answering the question and may even create an answer on the fly by combining relevant knowledge nuggets. Interpretation of questions using domain knowledge. Aggregation and composition of the answer.

Automated Content Tagging: To provide semantic tags that allow a document or other work-product to be "better known" by one or more systems so that search,

7 Based on Davis (2008).

integration or invocation of other applications becomes more effective. Tags are automatically inserted based on the computer analysis of the information, typically using natural language analysis techniques. A predefined taxonomy or ontology of terms and concepts is used to drive the analysis. Machine learning approaches based on statistical algorithms such as Bayesian networks.

Concept-based Search: To provide precise and concept-aware search capabilities specific to an area of interest using knowledge representations across multiple knowledge sources both structured and un-structured. Knowledge model provides a way to map translation of queries to knowledge resources.

Connection and Pattern Explorer: To discover relevant information in disparate but related sources of knowledge, by filtering on different combinations of connections or by exploring patterns in the types of connections present in the data. Inferences over models to identify patterns using the principles of semantic distance.

Content Annotation: To provide a way for people to add annotations to electronic content. By annotations we mean comments, notes, explanations and semantic tags. Knowledge model is used to assist people in providing consistent attribution of artefacts.

Context-aware Retriever: To retrieve knowledge from one or more systems that is highly relevant to an immediate context, through an action taken within a specific setting – typically in a user interface. A user no longer needs to leave the application they are in to find the right information knowledge model is used to represent context. This “profile” is then used to constrain a concept-based search.

Dynamic User Interface: To dynamically determine and present information on the web page according to user’s context. This may include related links, available resources, advertisements and announcements. Context is determined based on user’s search queries, web page navigation or other interactions she has been having with the system. A model of context and a memory of activities are used to control UI generation.

Enhanced Search Query: To enhance, extend and disambiguate user-submitted keyword searches by adding domain and context-specific information. For example, depending on the context a search query, “jaguar” could be enhanced to become “jaguar, car, automobile”, “jaguar, USS Star Trek”, “jaguar, cat, animal” or “jaguar, software, Schrödinger”. Knowledge models are used to express the vocabulary of a domain.

Expert Locator: To provide users with convenient access to experts in a given area who can help with problems, answer questions, locate and interpret specific documents, and collaborate on specific tasks. Knowing who is an expert in what can be difficult in an organization with a large workforce of experts. Expert Locator could also identify experts across organizational barriers. The profiles of experts are expressed in a knowledge model. This can then be used to match concepts in queries to locate experts.

Generative Documentation: To maintain a single source point for information about a system, process, product, etc., but deliver that content in a variety of forms, each tailored to a specific use. The format of the document and the information it contains are automatically presented as required by each particular audience. Knowledge model is used to represent formatting and layout. Semantic matching is a key component of the solution.

Interest-based Information Delivery: To filter information for people needing to monitor and assess large volumes of data for relevance, volatility or required response. The volume of targeted information is reduced based on its relevance according to a role or interest of the end user. Sensitive information is filtered according to the “need to know”. A profile of each user’s interests is expressed in a knowledge model. This is then be used to provide “smart” filtering of information that is either attributed with metadata or has knowledge surrogates.

Navigational Search; To use topical directories, or taxonomies, to help people narrow in on the general neighborhood of the information they seek. A taxonomy that takes into account user profiles, user goals and typical tasks performed is used to drive a search engine. To optimize information access by different stakeholders, multiple interrelated taxonomies are needed.

Product Design Assistant: To support the innovative product development and design process, by bringing engineering knowledge from many disparate sources to bear at the appropriate point in the process. Possible enhancements to the design process that result include rapid evaluation, increased adherence to best practices and more systematic treatment of design constraints.

Semantic Data Integrator: To allow data to be shared and understood across a variety of settings. Systems developed in different work-practice settings have different semantic structures for their data. Time-critical access to data is made difficult by these differences. A common knowledge model is used to provide one or more unified views of enterprise data. Typically this is done by using mapping. Rules are executed to resolve conflicts, provide transformations and build new objects from data elements.

Semantic Form Generator and Results Classifier: To improve data-collection process and data-input analysis by providing knowledge driven dynamic forms. A knowledge model is used to intelligently guide the user through data capture. The results are automatically classified and analysed according to the model

Semantic Service Discovery and Choreography: To enable increased reuse of existing services and the dynamic automation of processes through service composition and choreography. Knowledge models are used to enhance the functionality of service directories. Invocation methods, terminology and semantic description allow the dynamic discovery of services by machines.

Virtual Consultant: To offer a way for customers to define their individual goals and objectives, and then show them what products and services can help them meet those goals. Understanding customer's goals and requirements through a questionnaire or dialogue establishes a profile that helps you communicate effectively with them now and in the future.

Acknowledgments

Thank you very much, Lars and UILLD Programme committee for the opportunity to give a talk on this topic.

References

Baxley, Bob. 2003. "Universal Model of a User Interface." DOI: 10.1145/997078.997090. Accessed on 19 December 2014.

Bertalanffy, Ludwig von. 1972. "The history and status of general systems theory." *Academy of Management Journal* 15(4): 407–426.

Center for Universal Design. 2008 "About the Center: Ronald L. Mace." http://www.ncsu.edu/ncsu/design/cud/about_us/usronmace.htm. Accessed on 22 January 2015.

Davis, Mills. 2008. "Project10X's Semantic Wave 2008 Report: Industry Roadmap to Web 3.0 & Multibillion Dollar Market Opportunities." http://www.eurolibnet.eu/files/

REPOSITORY/20090507165103_SemanticWaveReport2008.pdf. Accessed on 19 December 2014.

Henriques, Gregg. 2003. "The Tree of Knowledge System and the Theoretical Unification of Psychology." *Review of General Psychology* 7(2):150–182.

Kim, Kab-Jin, Jae-Chul Lee, Sung-Min Ahn, Kang-Soo Lee, Chang-Won Lee, Young Jin Cho, Sunae Seo, Kyung-Ho Shin, Sug-Bong Choe and Hyun-Woo Lee. 2009. "Interdimensional universality of dynamic interfaces." *Nature* 458:740-742. http://www.nature.com/nature/journal/v458/n7239/full/nature07874.html. Accessed on 19 December 2014.

Maienborn, Claudia, Klaus von Heusinger and Paul Portner, eds. *Semantics: An International Handbook of Language Meaning*. Volume 1. Berlin: De Gruyter, 2011.

Sturgeon, Derrill L., Mark P. Vaughan and Christopher A. Howard. 2001. Universal user interface for a system utilizing multiple processes. US patent 6,219,041 filed 30 September 1997, and issued 17 April 2001. http://patents.com/us-6219041.html. Accessed on 19 December 2014.

Swanson, Don R. 2001. "On the Fragmentation of Knowledge, the Connection Explosion, and Assembling Other People's Ideas." *Bulletin of the American Society for Information Science and Technology* 27(3): 12–14. http://dx.doi.org/10.1002/bult.196. Accessed on 19 December 2014.

Wilson, Edward O. (2001). "How to Unify Knowledge." *Annals of the New York Academy of Sciences* 935(1): 12–17.

Emmanuelle Bermès

2 Following the User's Flow in the Digital Pompidou

Abstract: Since 2007, the Centre Pompidou, the major modern art museum in Paris, has developed a new digital strategy aiming at providing a global platform for online digital content: the Centre Pompidou Virtuel, which could literally translate as "Virtual Pompidou Centre" or more accurately "Digital Pompidou Centre". This platform provides access through a unique entry point to the whole digital production of the organization and associated institutions (Bpi, Ircam): digitized works of art, documents about art and art history, videos and podcasts, archival material, library books records, etc. The goal of the project was to make the online presence of the Centre Pompidou focus on the content rather than being just an institutional showcase mainly targeting physical visitors of the building in Paris. On the contrary, the Pompidou website is now an online reference tool for anyone interested in modern and contemporary arts, or in the humanities in general.

Keywords: Semantic web, Library linked data, User interfaces, User-generated content

Introduction

Since 2007, the Centre Pompidou, the major modern art museum in Paris, has developed a new digital strategy aiming at providing a global platform for online digital content: the Centre Pompidou Virtuel, which could literally translate as "Virtual Pompidou Centre" or more accurately "Digital Pompidou Centre". This platform provides access through a unique entry point to the whole digital production of the organization and associated institutions (Bpi, Ircam): digitized works of art, documents about art and art history, videos and podcasts, archival material, library books records, etc. The goal of the project was to make the online presence of the Centre Pompidou focus on the content rather than being just an institutional showcase mainly targeting physical visitors of the building in Paris. On the contrary, the Pompidou website is now an online reference tool for anyone interested in modern and contemporary arts, or in the humanities in general. Hence the Digital Pompidou is not about providing a virtual experience that would try to copy the onsite experience for visitors in our exhibitions, through an interface based on camera views like the Google Art Project.

First of all, we wanted to emphasise the diversity of our cultural activity, which doesn't rely only on the museum, but also involves conferences, live shows, cinema screenings and other live events involving artists of all kind.

Moreover, we're less interested in displaying what can already be seen than in revealing what is usually hidden. Among the 76,000 art works that are part of our museum collection, only about 2,000 are actually exhibited in the Paris building, in the course of temporary exhibitions or presentations of the permanent collection. The rest is either on loan or deposit in other places all around the world, or stored in the museum's storeroom.

Finally, the Centre Pompidou remains convinced that there is no way a virtual experience can replace the actual contact with works of art, the emotional and sensible approach to our cultural heritage. We hope that making more content available online will unveil new possibilities, either by making a new range of people come to the museum, or by allowing the display of forgotten works that wouldn't have been considered for exhibition had they not been digitized.

These statements led the Centre Pompidou to the definition of a broader scope, defining the "virtual" experience as something completely different from what can be seen onsite. This experience is based on the ability of our web users to create their own flow of meaning, by following links and aggregating content according to their own interests.

Traditional editorial approaches to online development in museums lead to emphasising only those works or artists that are considered of main interest, which results in the prevalence of a mainstream culture above more alternative forms of creation. Following the "long tail" paradigm, artists that are already well-known tend to have a heavier presence on museum websites than others. The Centre Pompidou is attached to its tradition of openness to new and alternative forms of arts and doesn't want to privilege a certain part of its collection, but rather to empower unexpected discoveries and serendipity.

In order to do so, the Centre Pompidou has created an online platform aggregating a great diversity of content, starting from the digitized works, which are the backbone of the website, but also including documents and archival material related to those works and their creators. Most of these digital resources were not created purposely for the website, but rather reflect the actual day-to-day activity of the Centre since its creation in 1977.

A large part of this content was actually already available on the former website, but it was scattered and hardly accessible for a user without a thorough knowledge of information retrieval techniques. In order to allow the average user to benefit from these hidden treasures, the Centre Pompidou adopted a semantic approach in the design of the new platform. The combination of semantic web technologies and an intense research on end user interface issues resulted in the creation of the Digital Centre Pompidou as it is today. But a lot of other possibilities are still waiting to be unveiled.

Why semantic web technologies?

One of the main challenges of the project lay in the creation of a global and common information space from data extracted from several databases which all have their own structure. We decided to adopt semantic web technologies in order to address this issue.

The Digital Centre Pompidou was created based on the aggregation of existing databases, which are used as management tools for the Centre's professionals in the course of their work. The main databases are:

- the Museum collection, a database dedicated to the management of the works of art and their curation; this database is based on a software shared with other French museums, called Videomuseum;
- the Agenda, a database which describes all the events (exhibitions, conferences, workshops, visits, etc.) past, present and future;
- the Library catalogues, based on traditional ILS systems (3 library collections are aggregated in the Digital Centre Pompidou: Bibliothèque Kandinsky, Bpi and Ircam);
- archives finding aids, both from the Centre Pompidou's institutional archive and from the Kandinsky library which holds several artists' fonds;
- audio-visual databases, usually based on local tools;
- other databases holding biographical information, journal articles, learning resources, shop products, etc.

It was a major challenge to be able to aggregate data from all those databases into one common interface for the public to search and browse. The data is very heterogeneous, as some of it follows library standards (MARC, MODS and Dublin Core), some archival standards (EAD for archives), some an internal locally defined structure (museum and audio-visual material) and part of this data even relates to entities that are not documents by nature (events, persons, etc.)

However, merging all this data reveals very interesting, as all those databases share common entities: for instance, if you're looking for Kandinsky, you could find interest in his paintings, the exhibitions that have shown his works, his archives held by the Kandinsky library, books and videos about him, photos of him in the archives, etc. All this information already exists in the different databases, but relating it in a consistent way still is a challenge.

In the course of the project, it was not our purpose to change the habits and tools of the professionals, so the principle of having separate databases was not a subject for discussions. Of course, a global change towards a digital-oriented purpose of the activity was needed, and led to new practices such as requesting authorization for online display when the content is copyrighted (which is almost always the case, as the Centre Pompidou preserves mainly art from the 20th and 21st centuries). Also, indexing the content of the resources was now necessary, as the idea of making those works accessible to the public at large also required different entry points from those used by professionals. However, beside these amendments to the way of describing things, very little change was induced by the project in terms of software or data models.

The new digital platform had to use these databases as sources, and aggregate and relate their content. As the data models were so different, the choice of semantic web technologies was almost natural.

Linked data offers a powerful way of achieving interoperability between databases of heterogeneous structure. In its final report (Baker et al. 2011), the Library Linked Data Incubator Group emphasises the relevance of these technologies for libraries, in particular in the perspective of interoperability across domains (libraries, archives, museums):

> The linked data approach offers significant advantages over current practices for creating and delivering library data while providing a natural extension to the collaborative sharing models historically employed by libraries. Linked data and especially linked open data is sharable, extensible, and easily re-usable. It supports multilingual functionality for data and user services, such as the labelling of concepts identified by language-agnostic URIs. These characteristics are inherent in the linked data standards and are supported by the use of Web-friendly identifiers for data and concepts. Resources can be described in collaboration with other libraries and linked to data contributed by other communities or even by individuals. Like the linking that takes place today between Web documents, linked data allows anyone to contribute unique expertise in a form that can be reused and recombined with the expertise of others. The use of identifiers allows diverse descriptions to refer to the same thing. Through rich linkages with complementary data from trusted sources, libraries can increase the value of their own data beyond the sum of their sources taken individually.
>
> By using linked open data, libraries will create an open, global pool of shared data that can be used and re-used to describe resources, with a limited amount of redundant effort compared with current cataloging processes.
>
> The use of the Web and Web-based identifiers will make up-to-date resource descriptions directly citable by catalogers. The use of shared identifiers will allow them to pull together descriptions for resources outside their domain environment, across all cultural heritage datasets, and even from the Web at large. Catalogers will be able to concentrate their effort on their domain of local expertise, rather than having to re-create existing descriptions that have been already elaborated by others.

> History shows that all technologies are transitory, and the history of information technology suggests that specific data formats are especially short-lived. Linked data describes the meaning of data ("semantics") separately from specific data structures ("syntax" or "formats"), with the result that linked data retains its meaning across changes of format. In this sense, linked data is more durable and robust than metadata formats that depend on a particular data structure.

The principles of linked data are designed to be applied to the web at large and across organizations, but they can also be fit for internal use within an institution or company: this kind of use is usually referred to as "Linked Enterprise Data" (LED) (Wood, 2010). LED is about applying linked-data principles and technology within the information system in order to increase interoperability between its components.

The four main principles of linked data are the following:

- use URIs as names for things;
- use HTTP URIs so that if someone looks up a URI he retrieves useful information;
- when someone looks up a URI, provide useful information using standards (RDF, SPARQL);
- provide links to other datasets.

The goal of these rules is to provide to the end user a seamless information space where he can "follow his nose" from one resource to the other, following their URIs, without the need to have any knowledge of their structure or storage. This form of interoperability should allow different institutions to publish their databases without knowledge of the software used by others, just as the Web allows web pages and websites to communicate through hypertext regardless of the storage of the pages on different servers and using different content management systems.

This is exactly the kind of interoperability that we wanted to build within the Centre Pompidou information system. We wanted a system that wouldn't enforce the data from the separate databases into one common structure, but still would make it possible to create links between the entities they share. As the museum professionals are very demanding in terms of data quality, we couldn't afford to lower the level of detail of the data by using only the lowest common denominator between the databases. The main advantage of the RDF model, with its triple structure and the use of URIs, is to bind together descriptions of entities of a great variety into a seamless data model.

The data model

The Digital Pompidou platform is based on an RDF core that binds together all the data from the different databases. They are thus expressed according to a common model using RDF and URIs. In order to handle this, an RDF ontology was created, based on a few main concepts: Work, Document, Person, Place, Collection, Event and Resource (Figure 2.1).

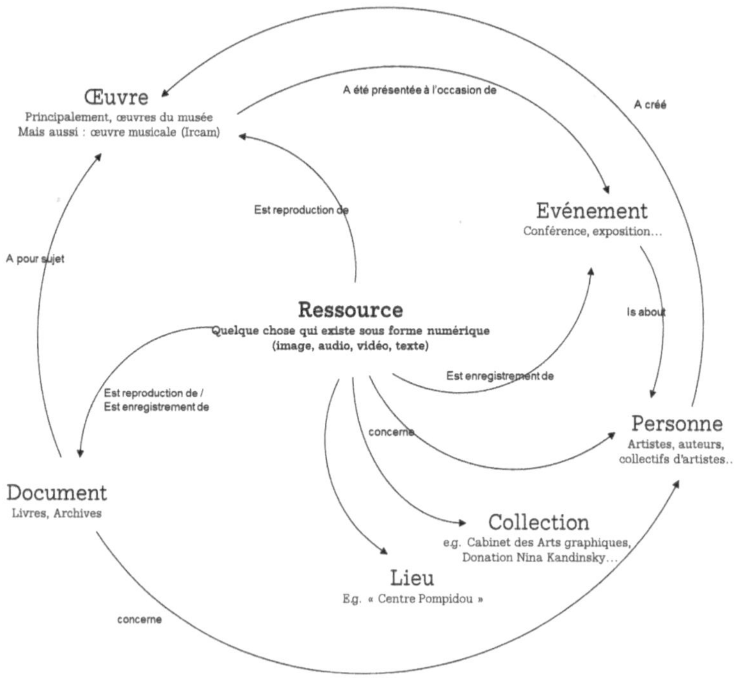

Figure 2.1: Overview of the Digital Pompidou data model

The main concepts are designed to integrate data from the different database sources: data from the Museum mainly relates to Works, Persons and Collections. The Agenda provides information about Events but also the Places where they are located. Data from libraries and archives is aggregated around the concept of Document. Finally, audio-visual material is provided as Resources together with information about the content of videos and audio recordings (Persons who are speaking during the conferences, Works that are presented, etc.). Art content (works from the Museum, recording of musical performances) is linked with event-based information (exhibitions, performances, conferences) and with other relevant resources (posters, photographs, books, archives, etc.) thus allowing to browse the website and discover all these resources in a serendipitous manner.

During this process, we learnt that it was quicker and easier to work with our own schema than try to adapt existing vocabularies, none of which were completely fit for our purpose due to the diversity of our resources. However, this was possible only as long as we intended to use the data within our own system and not to redistribute it to partners or make it available as open linked data. If we were to do so, which is definitely part of our plan for this year, we'd have to transform our local ontology into a standard one. Work has already been done in this respect, in collaboration with a class of students in documentation.

We also learnt that creating links between databases is not a trivial task, even if they are owned by the same institution and supposed to address similar topics. Entities such as Persons can be aligned using very simple keys such as given name plus family name. In most cases, the result is relevant because we are working on a narrow field of interest with little risk of ambiguity (there are, however, a few cases of homonyms). When it comes to Events or Works, it's a whole different story. Events often have very ambiguous names, and even taking into account the event's dates it's difficult to disambiguate, for instance, the name of an exhibition and the visit for disabled people to the same exhibition, or a series of conferences around the same topic. Works also have ambiguous names, and if you consider the collections from the Photography or Graphic Arts services, "sans titre" is probably the most frequent title in the database...

Moreover, those alignments have to be recreated each time the data is updated in the system, a process that happens every night for most of the data, as the website displays sensible information that requires frequent updates (ongoing events, data about people, right owners, etc.). Hence, even if we were able to edit the alignments manually, in order to disambiguate false positives for instance, the editing would be over-written by the next nightly update when the new source data comes in and erases the existing one.

In order to solve this issue, we worked to cross the identifiers from the different databases directly in the source databases. For instance, the audio-visual database has been enriched with a new data element which is the unique identifier for an event in the Agenda, imported from the latter. Using a specific interface, the people in charge of describing videos can pick up from a list the proper event the video is related to, in order to make sure that the link between the media and the event will be accurate. This kind of improvement requires evolutions of the source databases and the professionals' practice, even if it is only on the margin of their activity, but is important to ensure that the user experience will be consistent.

Finally, many of the links are still created manually by the Multimedia team which is in charge of curating the data for the website. Thanks to the RDF model, it is very easy to add links between resources. We use an editing interface called "RDF Editor" to create those links, which are basically triples binding existing URIs in our datastore. The RDF Editor then behaves like a new source database which only stores links. Those links are restored daily when the rest of the source data is updated. This process only requires that the URIs are persistent across updates.

The user interface

The purpose of the creation of this data model and all the links between the databases is to provide our users with a new experience: being able to browse the semantics of the data. The initial purpose of the project was to make it possible for users to retrieve our content, in particular art works, by using words from the natural language. A query such as "horse" would then retrieve not only those works of art that have the word "horse" in the title, but every representation of a horse thanks to iconographical indexing. This feature is offered in our website by the search engine SolR.

The creation of links also provides a very different way to browse the data. The interface has been designed to allow the presentation of many links on a single page. This required the use of design tricks such as the clickable tabs that unfold vertically to display more and more content. This presentation makes it possible to display all the related links to the resource, hence providing different points of view on the data:

- if a user is interested in a Work, they can discover the artist who created it, see different digitized versions, have access to audio-visual material such as an interview of the artist, or textual material like an article extracted from a printed catalogue. They can also discover in which previous exhibitions this work was shown, the place where it can be seen now, and browse a series of works ingested in the same collection.
- if the entry point of the user is the event, for instance if they want to see what exhibitions are ongoing currently in the Centre Pompidou, they have access to information about the event but also audio-visual material, recordings, the catalogue of the exhibition they can buy from the online shop or read at the library, discover related events such as visits for children or conferences, etc.

This ability to browse the graph according to one's own centre of interest is what we call "the flow of meaning": users extract their own meaning from the circulation in the graph of data; they build their own course adapting it to their interest and the time they want to spend on the website. Whereas in most websites circulation is mainly hierarchical, from the most general to the most specific, in the Digital Pompidou navigation takes the form of an hypertextual graph where all resources are displayed at the same level. Our website is also different from a traditional database in the sense that usually, you have to express a detailed query in order to reach a resource; if the query doesn't get you to what you're looking for, you would then try to reformulate it. Database records are often dead-ends, with no other choice than creating a new query to find other resources. On the contrary, the Digital Pompidou always offers links to other resources and allows broadening the search to things that were not looked for in the first place.

Before the website was officially launched, we conducted a user study to evaluate this new way of discovering content. We found out that our users did perceive that it was a completely new way of exploring data. They sometimes felt lost in the richness of the content, or had the impression that their browsing was circular; they looked for the site map and requested tools in order to help them visualize a location in this information space.

While expert users (academics, students) said they first had to spend a lot of time on the site in order to understand how it works, users who were just browsing the site out of curiosity liked the fact that they would get lost and discover unexpected resources. However, they often complained that they had found interesting resources but were not able to reproduce the path that had led them there, hence to retrieve the resource.

So it appears that we actually did succeed in creating a user interface that is completely original and specific to the fact that the underlying structure of the website is based on linked data. However, we need to develop new tools in order to help our users grasp the advantages of hyperlinked data and non-hierarchical models. This is what we intend to develop as a next step.

Perspectives for future development

We are currently working on a new version of the website that will bring some improvement to help our users with these aspects. In particular, the personal account will provide a "history" function and will record every resource that the user has displayed so that it will be easier for them to retrieve what they have already seen.

Future evolutions of the platform also include an even greater involvement of users in the construction of the meaning or semantics of the content, as we intend to offer collaborative tools for resources indexing and linking. This new feature will allow users to add keywords in a wiki-like interface, and thus create new paths to help find resources.

Integrating users' contributions into our data model, much alike the integration of several databases, is made easier by the fact that we're relying on a linked data model. Any addition to a resource can be managed as an RDF triple, a simple annotation to the content created by the Museum. Provenance information will need to be addressed in order to be able to keep the user generated content separate from the content that is validated by the institution.

Another interesting aspect of having an RDF core for our data is the fact that our current interface is only one of the infinite possibilities of presentation for the many links that we have created from our source data. The Digital Pompidou today provides the official interface displaying this data, but it's only one possible interpretation among many. We can predict that we'll work on a new design within 2 or 3 years, in order to improve the user experience, take into account the feedback we had and adapt to the new material that we're currently digitizing.

However, it would be interesting also to see what other actors could build by interpreting our data and in particular the added value that was created by the aggregation of databases that were distinct in the origin.

Data visualization has been explored for many years now, as an alternate way to provide access to large collections of data, but without succeeding in overcoming traditional interfaces such as textual search engines or mosaics made of small images. Now with the development of open data, big data and data journalism, a new interest emerges regarding these techniques, not so much as a querying tool that you would put into users hands but as a storytelling tool that can bring up new perspectives for your data. For instance, we could build a representation out of the Digital Pompidou's data presenting the links between artists based on the exhibitions that have shown their works.

Experiments have been conducted in this regard by IRI (Information technology Research Institute), a partner of Centre Pompidou on research in IT and digital developments. IRI has created HAD-Lab, a portal dedicated to learning resources in history of art for teachers. HAD-Lab experiments several interfaces for structured data, including a visualization tool that shows relationships created between different learning resources by tagging them with DBpedia URIs (Figure 2.2).

The important part of this idea is the storytelling: data visualization is only interesting if there is a story to illustrate or if it allows new stories to be discovered. The task of unveiling these stories can't be delegated to the users them-

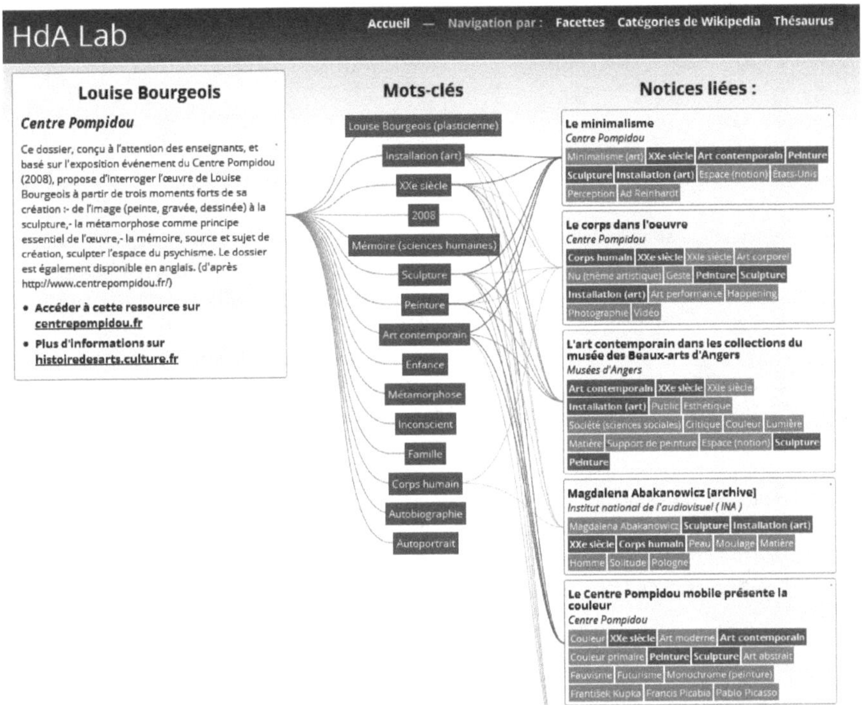

Figure 2.2: HDA-Lab visualization interface

selves, and information professionals such as librarians don't have experience in this area. For this reason, it is very important that other players (data journalists, data visualization experts or even artists) can have access to the raw data in order to be able to build their own representations, invent their own stories based on the material that we can provide.

During the summer of 2012, several experiments in data visualization were presented during the exhibition "Multiversités créatives" in the Centre Pompidou (Bernard 2012). The point was to demonstrate the added value of data visualization when it comes to understanding complex and moving structures such as the web. In the future, the Digital Pompidou should naturally become a source for this kind of experiments, thus providing a new perspective on the works and the artists presented in the museum.

In this perspective, the Digital Pompidou can be envisioned as an open door to a new interpretation of art and humanities. This tool will be even more powerful when the Pompidou data will be linked to external data such as Wikipedia, Freebase, VIAF or data.bnf.fr (Wenz 2010): this is definitely a motivation to open the data and make it available for others to create unexpected new interfaces with it.

References

Baker, Thomas, Emmanuelle Bermès, Karen Coyle, Gordon Dunsire, Antonie Isaac, Peter Murray, Michael Panzer, Jodi Schneider, Ross Singer, Ed Summers, William Waites, Jeff Young and Marcia Zeng. 2011. "Library Linked Data Incubator Group Final Report." http://www.w3.org/2005/Incubator/lld/XGR-lld-20111025/. Accessed on 19 December 2014.

Bernard, C.-R. 2012. "Multiversités créatives : Entretien avec Antonin Rohmer et Guilhem Fouetillou" [Video file]. http://www.centrepompidou.fr/cpv/ressource.action?param.id=FR_R-fcfa20aad7968c0c76cecc245537a6&param.idSource=FR_E-fbe91867c63213578548d4c568cb35a. Accessed on 19 December 2014.

Wenz, R., (2010). "data.bnf.fr: Describing Library Resources through an Information Hub. Presentation at the Semantic Web für Bibliotheken conference, 29–30 November 2010. [Video file]. http://scivee.rcsb.org/node/27093. Accessed on 19 December 2014.

Wood, David, ed. 2010. *Linking Enterprise Data*. New York: Springer. DOI: 10.1007/978-1-4419-7665-9. Accessed on 19 December 2014.

Patrick Le Bœuf

3 Customized OPACs on the Semantic Web

The OpenCat Prototype

Abstract: OpenCat is a research and development project that was led in 2012 by the National Library of France (hereafter referred to as BnF), in partnership with the public library of Fresnes (a small town located in the suburbs of Paris), and the French software editor company named Logilab, which specializes in semantic web technologies.[1] The initial objective of this project was to enable a small library to take advantage of the publication of (part of) the content of BnF's catalogues as semi-FRBRized linked open data on the data.bnf.fr web site to enrich its own catalogue with the result of that semi-FRBRization process, along with snippets from external information resources. The outcome is a Semantic Web application that makes it possible for libraries to share the same dump of FRBRized linked data, while they can customize the way it is displayed to end users and enriched with external information.

This paper will focus first on the data.bnf.fr project, which occasioned the OpenCat project and formed the basis for it; then CubicWeb, the technical platform that served to build the OpenCat prototype, will be briefly introduced; some features of the OpenCat prototype will be described; and lastly, some responses to the prototype from a panel of end users will be analysed.

Keywords: Bibliographic data as linked open data, OPACs and Library linked data, Data aggregation

Introduction

In the summer of 2011, BnF launched a new web site, named data.bnf.fr.[2] This web site, which was awarded the Stanford Prize for Innovation in Research Libraries (SPIRL) in 2013,[3] was the outcome of over one year of efforts to find ways

1 For more information on the three partners in this project, see, respectively: http://www.bnf.fr, http://bm.fresnes94.fr/, and http://www.logilab.fr/. (Accessed on 20 December 2014.) This project was supported by the French Ministère de la Culture et de la Communication.

2 http://data.bnf.fr. Accessed on 20 December 2014.

3 For more information, see: http://library.stanford.edu/projects/stanford-prize-innovation-research-libraries-spirl/bibliothèque-nationale-de-france-judges. Accessed on 20 December 2014.

to make BnF's resources more visible on the web and to transform the metadata that describes them into linked open data available for anyone to re-use.[4]

BnF has two catalogues, *BnF catalogue général* for published resources (http://catalogue.bnf.fr),[5] and *BnF archives et manuscrits* for archival collections and unique manuscripts (http://archivesetmanuscrits.bnf.fr), plus several databases that describe particular types of items or that focus on particular features of items otherwise described at a lesser level of granularity in either of the two main catalogues. In addition to that, BnF also has a digital library, Gallica (http://gallica.bnf.fr), which derives its descriptive metadata from the two main catalogues, and web pages that correspond to BnF's activities in the field of cultural mediation, such as "virtual exhibitions" (http://expositions.bnf.fr) or recorded lectures (http://www.bnf.fr/fr/evenements_et_culture/conferences_en_ligne.html). All these tools, although they share the same general objective of enabling end users to discover BnF's resources, have separate interfaces, as they are built on different formats: *BnF catalogue général* uses a specific instantiation of the MARC family of formats, named INTERMARC; *BnF archives et manuscrits* is produced using the EAD DTD; and the metadata that serves to retrieve digitized items on Gallica is expressed in Dublin Core. The data.bnf.fr project originated from the urgent need to propose a common interface allowing end users to query all these information repositories at once, while preserving the distinct structure, granularity, and ontological commitment of each of them individually.

The data.bnf.fr web site (http://data.bnf.fr) consists of human-readable pages, the content of which is also available as RDF and JSON declarations in order to be exploited by semantic web applications. The objective is not to *substitute* this web site for the dedicated interfaces of the BnF's existing catalogues, but to provide web users who are not accustomed to searching the BnF's resources with a pivot interface that digs such resources out from the deep web (hence the need for human-readable pages), in addition to making bibliographic information available as linked open data (hence the need for RDF and JSON declarations). The RDF and JSON declarations are provided under the French government's open licence, which is very similar to the Creative Commons CC-BY licence. Indeed, the content of the data.bnf.fr database represents the first and, to this day, most significant data set that has been made available from the French platform for public open data, data.gouv.fr (http://www.data.gouv.fr/DataSet/30383137).

4 The conceptual model that lies at the heart of the data.bnf.fr database is available, in a simplified form, from: http://data.bnf.fr/semanticweb-en#Ancre3. Accessed on 20 December 2014.

5 All URLs given in the text were accessed on 20 December 2014.

As of 1 July 2014, the data.bnf.fr site comprised over 714,000 pages, divided up into three main categories: Authors, Works, and Topics.[6] Each page is devoted to a single author, work, or topic, and includes brief citations of bibliographic records associated with that author, work, or topic; these brief citations are provided with links that lead web users into the BnF's catalogues. "Work" is not to be understood here in the sense Bibframe uses it, but in the FRBR sense of the term. This concept was chosen as a convenient collocating unit for bibliographic data, because the articulation between a cultural object (such as a novel, a poem, a scientific study, a symphony or a motion picture), its variants (be they compositional, linguistic, performatory, etc.), and the many ways these variants can be packaged for dissemination within a society, was deemed to have a broader significance than just as a construct of the entity-relationship model designed by IFLA for bibliographic data in the 1990s. Indeed, we regard it as having been the implicit underlying conceptualization of the bibliographic universe for at least two centuries. We think that these distinctions lie at the heart of the definition of networks of cultural objects, even in the semantic web era. Unlike some "FRBR sceptics" who have recently appeared and who argue that FRBR is not compatible with the very spirit of linked open data, we believe that the fact that not all other communities outside libraries are aware of the FRBR model or willing to implement it should not induce librarians to refrain from using it to inform the underlying structure of the linked open data they produce. We feel encouraged in this direction by the existence of Wikipedia pages devoted to "Works", which proves that even in the 21st century it still makes sense to organize a cultural discourse around the notion of works, rather than to content oneself with listing myriads of publications defined on the basis of the ISBN criterion only. We are also convinced that the FRBR distinction between Work, Expression, and Manifestation can actually facilitate, rather than hinder, the linking functionality within the web of data, as it allows other communities to re-use indifferently either the complete RDF graph (from the Manifestation level to the Work level) that describes a given publication, or just that part of it that relates to the specific level they may be interested in and find relevant for their own needs, e.g., just the information that pertains to the Work and Expression levels. From a pragmatic point of view, taking the FRBR Work entity as its collocating unit for exposing bibliographic data as linked open data also enables the data.bnf.fr web site to not simply duplicate the catalogue and result in millions of atomic pages, but to organize bibliographic information in a way that makes sense for end users because it corresponds to the way they envision cultural history.

6 Two further categories are represented: Years, and Places.

At its current stage of development, however, the data.bnf.fr project does not propose a complete implementation of the FRBR model. It can be more aptly labelled a semi-FRBRized view of the BnF's catalogues than a fully FRBRized one. At the time being, due to the nature of the legacy data that has to be transformed into linked open data, the Expression entity is not represented in the data.bnf.fr web pages, but it is included in the plan for future development. As other experimentations in FRBRization, such as OCLC's FictionFinder, have amply demonstrated, the Expression entity, although it is the most "natural" and self-evident in the FRBR model, is also the one that proves most difficult to be dug up from legacy data – an interesting issue from the point of view of the philosophy of cultural history.

The data.bnf.fr structure elaborates on the authority work already performed in the BnF's catalogues. Authority records are created at the BnF for all musical works that are available in notated form, all "art music" (as opposed to both folk and popular music) works that are available as sound recordings, all literary works that are mentioned in the IFLA lists of "anonymous classics",[7] and all works of any type whenever a controlled access point based on the uniform title that identifies them is needed for subject indexing. The data.bnf.fr "Work" pages are automatically generated from those authority records, and bibliographic records that, in the catalogues, are not associated with them (most often because they describe publications of works for which an authority record is only usable as part of a subject access point) are aligned on them through specific algorithms. As of 1 July 2014, the data.bnf.fr web site contained links to 7 million bibliographic records, i.e., one fifth of the records present in *BnF catalogue général*. Over 70% of web users who visit one of the data.bnf.fr web pages follow the links to other web pages created by the BnF (either the catalogues or the digital library), which is a good indication that the data.bnf.fr web site is rather successful as a way of making library resources "alluring" to web users who were previously unaware of libraries' potential for their information needs. But the main objective pursued when publishing linked open data is not just to have it read, but to have it re-used by others who should feel free to do whatever they want with it. We are aware of several cases in which the content of the data.bnf.fr web pages was actually re-used by developers who are totally independent from the BnF, e.g., the mobile application named CatBNF which makes it possible to browse the data.bnf.fr pages on an iPhone or an iPod, or the web site named IF Verso, which is devoted to the notion of translation and proposes a catalogue of translations from the

7 http://www.ifla.org/node/4957. Accessed on 20 December 2014.

French based on the Work-centred structure of the data.bnf.fr web site.[8] However, there may be other re-use cases of which we are not aware, as of course the difficulty with the freedom enabled by linked open data is precisely that it is very difficult to keep track of all the transformations undergone by the bibliographic data thus exposed.

The CubicWeb application framework, or, the semantic web seen as a construction game

The data.bnf.fr application was built using the application framework named CubicWeb, which has been developed by the French software editor company Logilab since 2001 (version 2 was released in 2006 and the current version, version 3, has been downloadable for free since 2008).[9] CubicWeb is devoted to semantic web techniques used as a means to federate data sets from heterogeneous sources and display them in a variety of ways corresponding to clients' various needs. CubicWeb was designed as a generic platform consisting of components that can be re-used and rearranged in various combinations so that the time and cost of developing specific applications can be reduced. In CubicWeb's parlance, these components are called "cubes", because they consist of three elements: a data model that is expressed in the formalism of an entity-relationship schema, the logic that is required in order to manipulate the data, and the view code that makes it possible to visualize the federated data (user interface, export in various standards). The query language used by CubicWeb is RQL (Relation Query Language), is similar to W3C's query language SPARQL, and is closely related to the underlying data model.[10] This structure makes it possible to provide access to resources that are deemed useful for end users, and that are identified by more or less perennial, dereferenceable URIs.

Since the data.bnf.fr application and web site were developed by the Logilab company, and since the objective of the OpenCat project was to explore the possibility of federating bibliographic data from the data.bnf.fr pages, local holdings

8 CatBNF: http://www.appdata.com/ios_apps/apps/3998491-catbnf/26-france. Accessed on 3 January 2015; IF Verso: http://ifverso.com/. Accessed on 20 December 2014.

9 Documentation about CubicWeb is available in: "Logilab, CubicWeb – the Semantic Web is a Construction Game!". http://docs.cubicweb.org/. Last updated on 18 September 2012. Accessed on 20 December 2014.

10 For more information about the way CubicWeb is used for the data.bnf.fr project, see Simon, Wenz, Michel and Di Mascio 2013.

data, and other types of data from external sources in a single customized OPAC, it was quite logical for the Logilab company to propose itself as the third partner in that project.

Some features of the OpenCat prototype, or, a national library's open data at the service of a local library

The initiative of proposing the OpenCat project emanated in November 2011 from the Fresnes municipal library. This initiative was quite consistent with a deeply rooted tradition there, as this library had been publicly advocating and internally implementing for a number of years a proactive policy aiming at reducing cataloguing time and costs by re-using both the authority and bibliographic records produced by BnF (Giappiconi 1998). The six objectives of the project were introduced in the library's proposal as follows:

1. facilitate the search for documents by displaying query results organized around the FRBR notion of "Work";
2. use semantic web techniques to combine in a single hit list documents from various sources;
3. propose direct links to freely accessible digitized documents whenever possible;
4. enrich hit lists with contextual information taken from Open Data repositories;
5. propose a new approach to subject browsing through an intuitive graphic representation of the RAMEAU subject indexing language indexed as SKOS, and
6. use in the library world the same techniques and services as in commercial sites.

This proposal was received favourably by BnF, as it was immediately regarded there as a convenient means "to ensure that the way the BnF envisions the future of its metadata will ultimately meet practical needs and constraints from the national public library network rather than propose a scheme that nobody would use" (Illien 2012, 9–10).

The OpenCat project was officially launched in May 2012, and was to last fifteen months. By early November 2012, Logilab already had delivered a first prototype. The current version of this prototype is publicly available from http://

demo.cubicweb.org/opencatfresnes, with all the data that is relevant for the Fresnes library. Another experimental version is being tested. It contains data from other libraries in addition to Fresnes, displays extended functionalities, and has links to a larger array of external web sites; however, access to that version is restricted through login and password. A password is given to any library that wishes to experiment the addition of local holdings information to the contents of OpenCat.

The first step consisted of developing a first data model and merging into one repository data sets from both BnF and the Fresnes library, plus data sets from external sources with the aim of enriching the catalogue. The data set from the Fresnes library did not comprise the entire catalogue of that library, but only that portion thereof corresponding to works present in the data.bnf.fr database. This portion represents about 4,000 bibliographic records out of the 230,000 that were copied in the data repository hosted by Logilab; these 4,000 bibliographic records describe manifestations of about 3,000 out of the 45,000 works to which a data.bnf.fr page is devoted.

The second step consisted of developing graphic mock-ups and a demonstrator that allowed the project team to perform tests on the available data, refine the data model, and select the navigation scenarios and functionalities that were deemed the most relevant among a number of proposed alternatives. What follows is a brief guided tour of that demonstrator.

The homepage of the public prototype consists of three sections: (a) a Google-like search box in which users can enter any kind of terms, (b) random proposals of digitized items, and (c) an automatically produced timeline of works that were granted a literary award (Figure 3.1, p. 38).

When users type the term "Émile Zola" in the search box, a list of suggestions is automatically displayed. This list includes the name of a composer who collaborated with Émile Zola, the title of a work by Émile Zola, and names of characters imagined by Émile Zola and for which a subject authority record exists, and the complete controlled access point for Émile Zola (Figure 3.2, p. 39).

It is also possible to bypass the list of suggestions, and launch the query without having to select one of the items in the list. In that case, the system returns a list of hits, with the possibility to refine the query, by picking a category of information, such as: person, corporate body, topic, title of work (Figure 3.3, p. 39).

If a user looks for the name "Eugène Ionesco", they will find some information elements from the authority record produced by the BnF, combined (without any manual intervention by the user) with a link to the data.bnf.fr page devoted to Ionesco, an excerpt from the biographical note devoted to Ionesco on the web site of the Académie française, of which he was a member, and a link to the rest of the page from which that excerpt was taken. This biographic information is followed

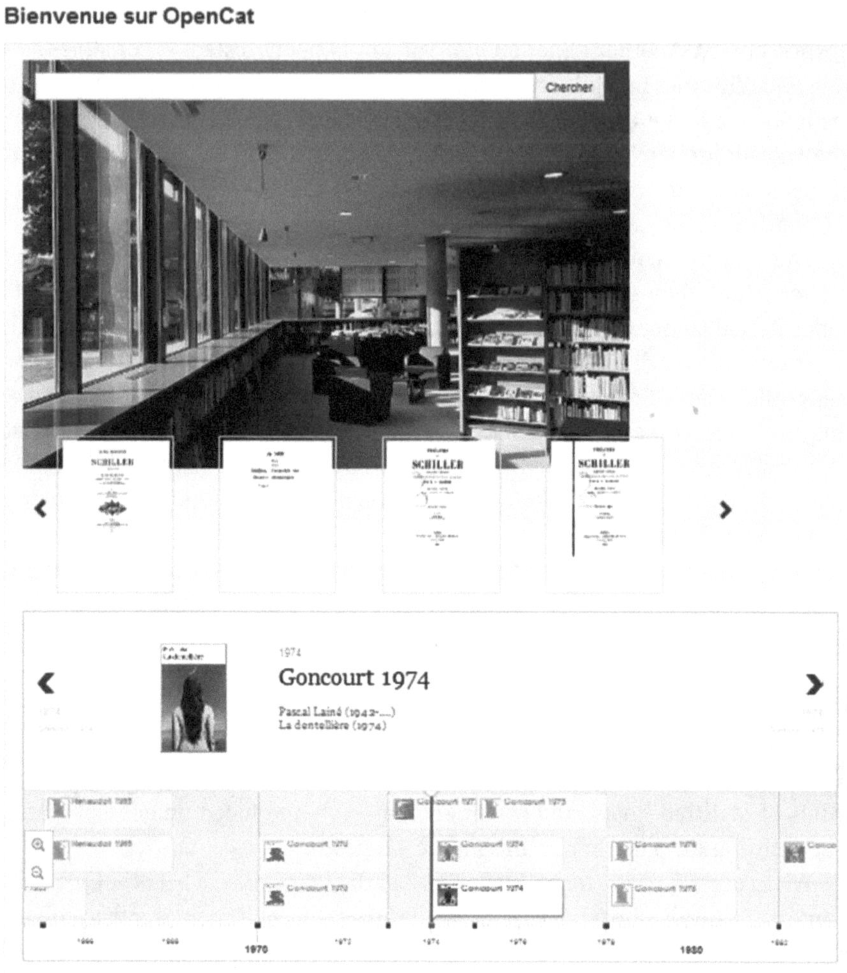

Figure 3.1: OpenCat Homepage

by three distinct sections: (a) Ionesco's works, organized along a timeline according to the date of their first publication, (b) Ionesco's works, organized as a list of clickable links to pages devoted to them, and (c) links to "other resources", in this case a virtual exhibition prepared by the National Library of France (Figure 3.4, p. 40).

The experimental version of the prototype shows, in addition to all of the above, a link to the speech delivered by Ionesco when he joined the Académie française, links to pages devoted to Ionesco's contemporaries (in the future, it

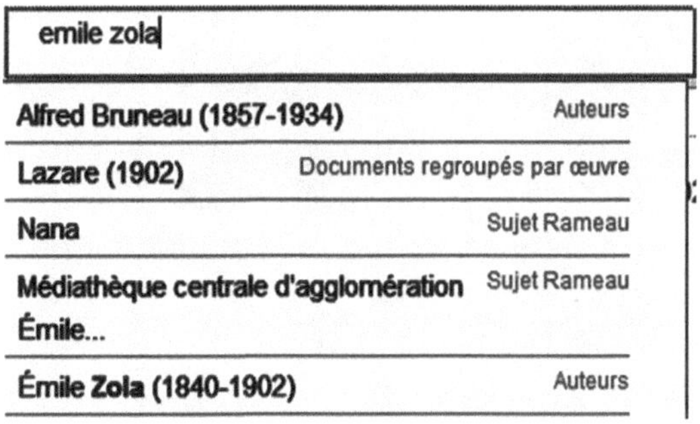

Figure 3.2: List of suggestions for a query on Émile Zola

Figure 3.3: Refining a query after the initial list of suggestions was bypassed

will be possible to replace this strictly chronological connection with more meaningful ones, such as other authors who were active in the same field of interest, or who wrote works belonging to the same genre), and links to popular web sites such as DBpedia, FreeBase, MusicBrainz or Flickr (Figure 3.5, p. 41).

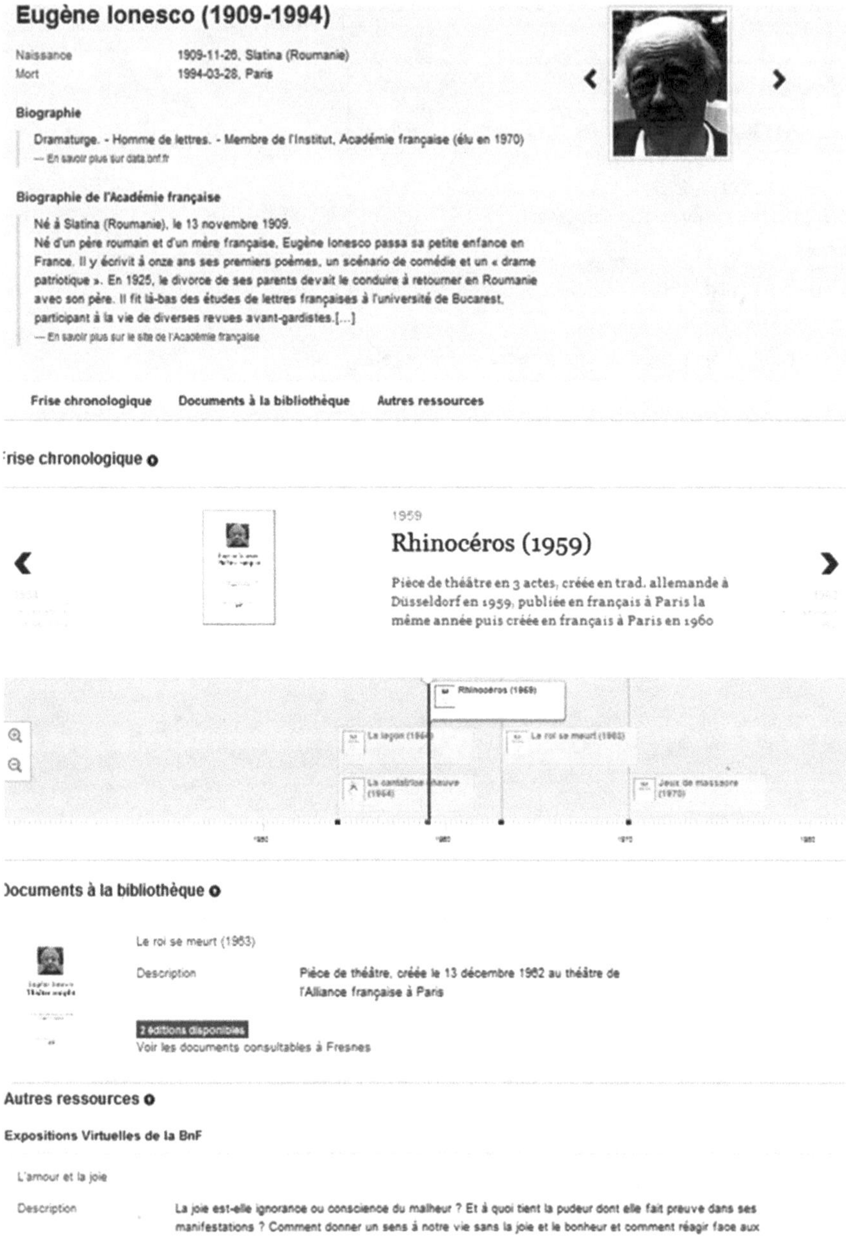

Figure 3.4: Author page for Eugène Ionesco in OpenCat (adapted)

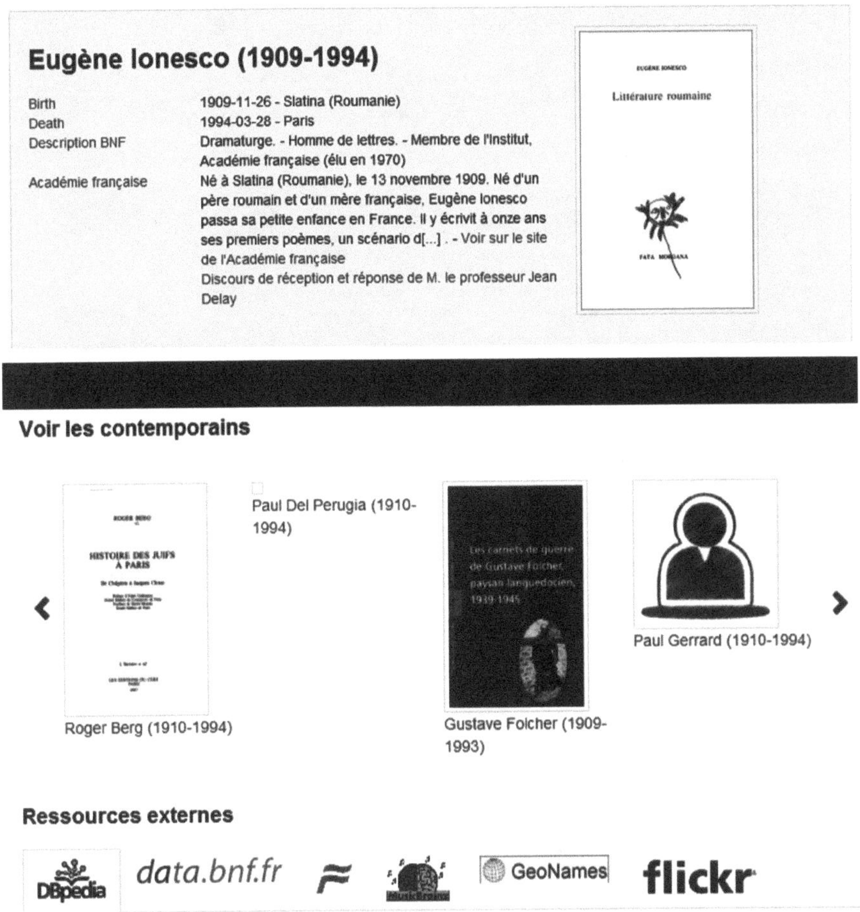

Figure 3.5: Author page for Eugène Ionesco in the experimental version

A user who types the term "Pathelin" in the search box will obtain a page devoted to the anonymous mediaeval work *Farce de maître Pierre Pathelin* that contains a summary of the work, taken from a commercial web site; a list of the seven editions of which the library holds a copy, and links to nine digitized items available from Gallica, the BnF's digital library (Figure 3.6, p. 42).

If a user types the term "Hamlet" in the search box, the OpenCat demonstrator will display a list of various suggestions, including the play entitled *Hamlet*, the subject heading for the Ophelia character, and the subject heading for the Elsinore castle (Figure 3.7, p. 43).

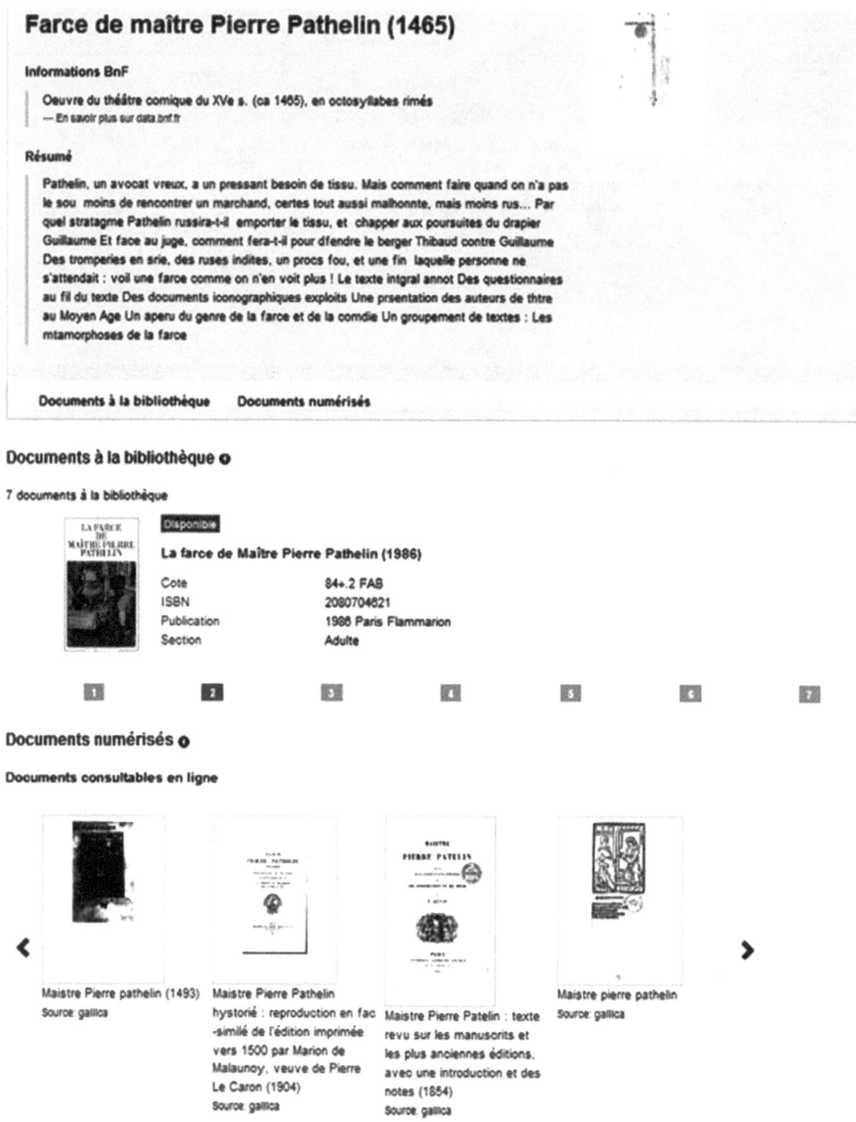

Figure 3.6: Work page for an anonymous work

If a user types the term "poésie", the demonstrator will display a list of poets and poetic works from which to pick (Figure 3.8, p. 43).

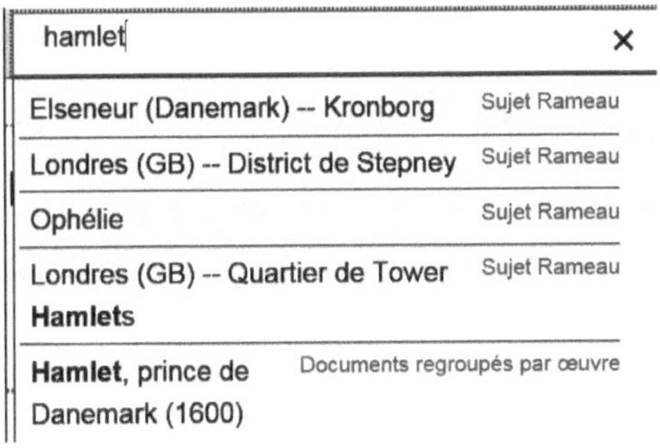

Figure 3.7: List of suggestions for a query on Hamlet

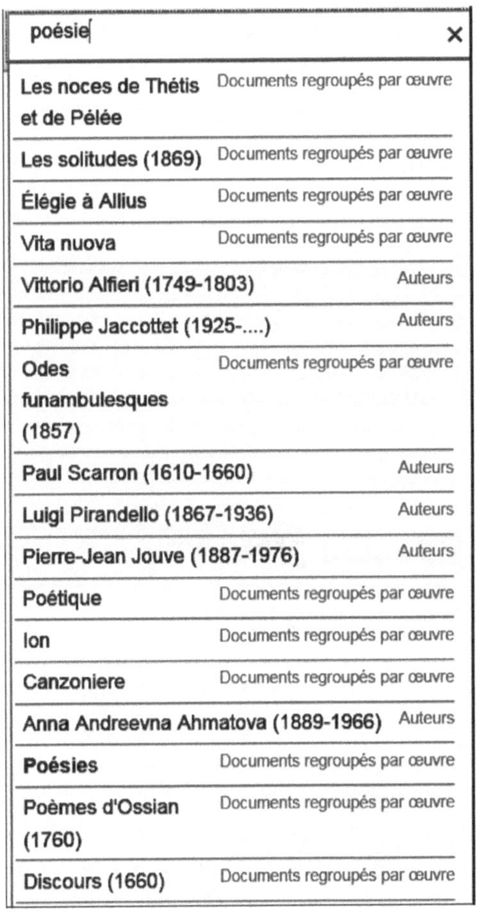

Figure 3.8: List of suggestions for a query on “poésie” on OpenCat

The public version of the prototype does not allow one to search by subject, but the experimental one provides access to information taken from the subject authority file maintained by Centre national RAMEAU (hosted by the National Library of France and available from the data.bnf.fr site), links to associated bibliographic records, and links to external resources. For instance, a query on the term “jeunesse” (youth) leads users to a number of recorded lectures available from Canal-U (an academic network web site).

If a user types the ISBN 978-2-81000-220-7, OpenCat will return the work *Madame Bovary*, an edition of which is identified by this ISBN, although the Fresnes library does not hold any copy of that specific edition. This is made possible by the fact that, in the data.bnf.fr database, all editions of *Madame Bovary* are collocated on the page devoted to that work. It is therefore possible to imagine that the catalogue, in the future, will be able to notify users that the library holds no copy of the edition they searched under its ISBN, but that another edition of the same work is available to them (Figure 3.9).

Figure 3.9: Suggestion for a query on an ISBN

Figure 3.10 (p. 45) indicates the sources from which information is aggregated in OpenCat.

Some responses to the OpenCat prototype

In December 2012, ten patrons of the Fresnes library, aged between 34 and 63, were asked to test the OpenCat prototype. They were left free to discover it by themselves for fifteen minutes, after just a very brief presentation of its main functionalities. Then their opinions about that experimentation were collected by one member of the BnF staff and one member of the Fresnes library staff, who asked them to try a specific query on a predetermined topic that was known to highlight the main features of the prototype that it was important to assess. All panellists expressed their satisfaction that the traditional content of a library catalogue was enriched with information from external sources. However, this enrichment was also perceived as possibly blurring the identity and the very nature of the interface: some panellists felt that there was either too much information for a local

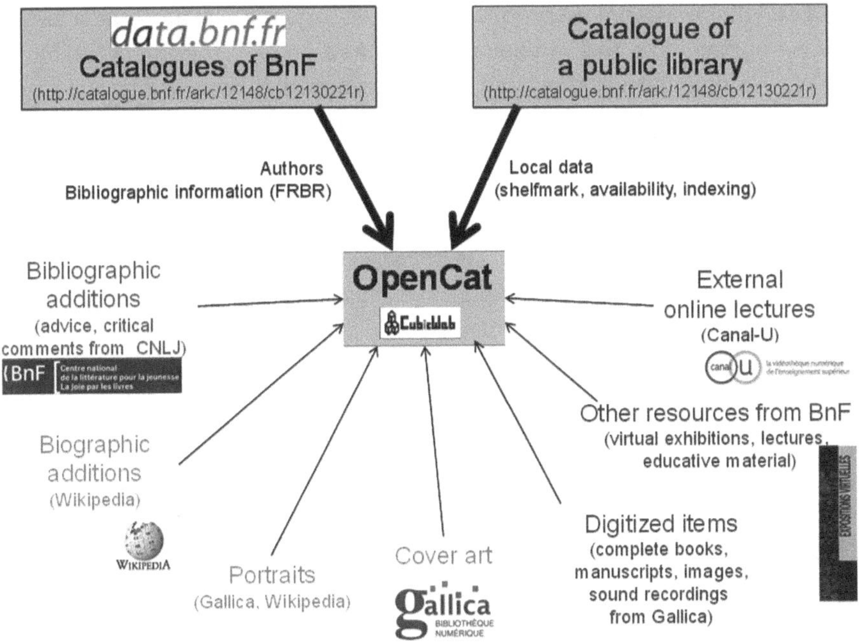

Figure 3.10: Sources for the information aggregated in OpenCat

library catalogue, or not enough of it for an online encyclopedia. Inevitably, comparisons were drawn with Wikipedia.

On the whole, the panellists were satisfied with the ergonomics and ease of navigation of the prototype. However, the autocomplete function of the search box was perceived as too constraining and the order in which the proposed items are listed as illogical; none of the panellists seems to have discovered by themselves that it is actually possible to bypass that list of suggestions.

The presence of biographical data about the authors was felt as a noticeable improvement. None of the panellists thought that the presence of links to external sites was irrelevant, though they found it disturbing that the content of the linked pages was not displayed in a new window but substituted to the page on which they had clicked, making it difficult then to realize that they had left the catalogue. They experienced some difficulty in returning to the OpenCat interface after they had followed links to external sites.

Oddly enough, none of the panellists made any comment on the fact that all the editions of a given work are gathered under the uniform title of that work. Perhaps we can regard this absence of particular comments as an indication that this way of organizing bibliographic information was felt by the panellists as so "natural" that it was not even worth noticing it. Perhaps, in spite of the reduced number of panellists, this can be interpreted as a proof of concept of the FRBR model, showing that searching and identifying a work is perceived by end users as more important than searching and identifying a specific manifestation, the title of which may reveal nothing as to the various works that can be embodied in it. A data model that would content itself with repeating the manifestation title at the work level would therefore be likely to be deemed inefficient in terms of convenience of the user whenever a manifestation contains more than one work. One of the panellists suggested that a page devoted to a given author should list not just that author's works, but also works derived by other authors from that author's works – an indication that even complex bibliographic relationships are of interest to library patrons without any training in cataloguing, and that simplistic views about bibliographic information might well miss the point.

Follow-up and future developments

Although the OpenCat project is not over yet, other local libraries have already expressed their interest in participating in similar projects. The public libraries of Saône-et-Loire (a French department located in Burgundy) want to use OpenCat to build a union catalogue at the department level. The idea would be that each individual library in the local network could keep their own internal management system, while sharing a common OPAC based on OpenCat that would provide access to a common dump of semi-FRBRized bibliographic data from the data.bnf.fr web site. Information relating to the availability status of the holdings of each library would be added to that dump, making it possible for end users to reserve a document from their mobile phone.

OpenCat can therefore be regarded as a promising project that opens new potentials for library collaboration at the national level. Logilab intends to develop another demonstrator, which will allow libraries to test the display of a selection of records from their catalogue, in order to show that the prototype was not designed to be used by the Fresnes library only but that any library can have it customized in order to meet their needs.

OpenCat was not designed as a tool for creating bibliographic data, but for displaying pre-existing bibliographic data on the Web in a manner that is likely to enhance its usability. It is not a cataloguing tool, but a tool that enables local libraries to customize a common OPAC that provides access to bibliographic data produced at the national level, and holdings data produced at the local level. With OpenCat, BnF made the strategic choice of disseminating its data in a formalism that is compliant with the semantic web, even before the production tool that serves to create it was changed.

The advantage of OpenCat is that local libraries can implement it without having to change their ILS. This possibility allows for a period of transition before all libraries of a given country can evolve from a MARC environment to a semantic web environment.

References

Giappiconi, Thierry. 1998. "Les ressources bibliographiques de la Bibliothèque nationale de France: la politique bibliographique de la bibliothèque de Fresnes" *Bulletin des bibliothèques de France* 43(6): 26–33.

Illien, Gildas. 2012. "Are You Ready to Dive in? A Case for Open Data in National Libraries." Paper Presented at the IFLA World Library and Information Congress, Helsinki 2012. http://conference.ifla.org/past-wlic/2012/181-illien-en.pdf. Accessed on 20 December 2014

Simon, Agnès, Romain Wenz, Vincent Micheland Adrien Di Mascio. 2013. "Publishing Bibliographic Records on the Web of Data: Opportunities for the BnF (French National Library)." In *The Semantic Web: Semantics and Big Data, 10th International Conference, ESWC 2013, Montpellier, France, May 26–30 2013: Proceedings*, edited by Philipp Cimiano, Oscar Corcho, Valentina, Presutti, Laura Hollink, Sebastian Rudolph, 563–577. Berlin: Springer. doi:10.1007/978-3-642-38288-8_38. http://eswc-conferences.org/sites/default/files/papers2013/simon.pdf . Accessed on 20 December 2014.

Ryan Shaw, Patrick Golden and Michael Buckland

4 Using Linked Library Data in Working Research Notes

Abstract: We describe how we are experimenting with using linked library data to connect the organizational infrastructures of libraries, archives, and special collections with those of researchers who use them. The site of this experimentation is Editors' Notes, an open-source hosted service for organizing the library and archives-based research of documentary editors. We report on an initial trial of incorporating linked data from libraries and other sources into Editors' Notes, and describe how that trial has informed our current effort to usefully exploit linked data to benefit researchers. We conclude with an overview of the potential benefits.

Keywords: Linked data, Digital humanities, Note-taking

Introduction

Documentary editing projects prepare "editions" of documents such as letters, diaries, and essays that have value as evidence for political, intellectual, or social history (Kline and Perdue 2008, 2). These projects rely heavily on libraries, archives, and special collections as they research the people, places, organizations, events and ideas referenced in the documents they are editing. This research is organized in the form of "working notes" organized around particular questions. These notes are eventually distilled into footnotes in a published "edition" of historical documents.

The published footnotes represent just a small fraction of the research produced by documentary editing projects. The majority of the research produced by editors and their assistants is represented by the working notes they develop to answer questions raised by their documents. These working notes are typically created during the course of researching a particular question and the specific forms they take may vary with the work practices of individual researchers. For example, consider a specific documentary editing project: the Margaret Sanger Papers Project (MSPP) at New York University, which has since 1985 been editing and publishing the papers of American birth-control pioneer Margaret Sanger.[1] A letter from an Indian birth-control activist to Sanger may raise some questions

1 http://www.nyu.edu/projects/sanger/. Accessed on 23 December 2014.

in an MSPP editor's mind regarding the activist's role in planning a conference on birth control held in Sweden. The editor decides that some research is needed to better understand her role and the other people and organizations involved, and so she creates a "working note" to track this research (Figure 4.1). She structures the note as an annotated bibliography, with an entry for each resource found to contain useful information, and including both a bibliographic description of the resource and a summary of the information found.

Figure 4.1: A documentary editor's "working note" about an Indian birth-control activist's role in planning the Fourth International Conference on Planned Parenthood.

In addition to this annotated bibliography, there may be a summary distilling all the relevant information found in the various sources. This distillation forms the basis for the eventual published footnote. But it is very likely that the working note contains a variety of useful information that will not appear in the published footnote due to either lack of space or unresolved issues with the information. Working notes may include doubts about published accounts; known false leads; promising clues and lines of inquiry that might be followed up later; notes that someone else knows about some point; references to documents not yet located; citations known to be garbled; unresolved queries; and so on.

The MSPP editors seek to communicate the value of the documents they edit by contextualizing them, identifying and explaining within footnotes the people, places, organizations, events and ideas that documents' authors refer to or imply.

Dhanvanthi Rama Rau and the Fourth ICPP are two such topics. In the published edited volumes, these various topics are linked to each other and to sources in libraries and archives via a rich web of explanation and commentary. So while editorial projects are nominally organized around the "papers" of a single historical figure, such as Sanger, projects end up carrying out in-depth research surrounding their studied era, reaching well beyond the narrow scope of their central figure's biography.

As they look for relevant documents, researchers use the catalogues and finding aids created and maintained by librarians and archivists. But once researchers have found those relevant documents, they begin creating working notes and bibliographic data in separate organizing systems. Sophisticated researchers, such as those involved in documentary editing projects, may even construct structured compilations of data such as chronologies and name authorities. These systems could conceivably benefit from re-using data from catalogues and finding aids, but in practice this rarely happens.

This paper describes our ongoing effort to provide useful working tools for library- and archives-based research and our experiments with integrating linked data from libraries and other sources into these tools. First we provide some background describing the kinds of tools three documentary editing projects—the MSPP, the Emma Goldman Papers (EGP),[2] and the Elizabeth Cady Stanton & Susan B. Anthony Papers Project (ECSSBAP)[3]—currently use to organize their research. Then we discuss some of the problems with these tools, and introduce Editors' Notes, an open-source hosted service designed to address these problems. We report on an initial experiment with incorporating into Editors' Notes linked data from libraries and other sources, and describe how that experiment has informed our current effort to usefully exploit linked data to benefit researchers. We conclude with an overview of what we expect those benefits to be.

Current tools for organizing editorial research

Editorial projects rely on a mix of technologies to organize and manage their working notes and bibliographic data. While some projects still rely on handwritten notes, the general trend among the projects we have worked with has been away from paper pads towards scanned documents and typed notes. As is the case with most historians, documentary editors typically organize their notes

2 http://sunsite.berkeley.edu/goldman/. Accessed on 23 December 2014.
3 http://ecssba.rutgers.edu/. Accessed on 23 December 2014.

in topically organized folders (Rutner and Schofield 2012). These folders reside in the project's filing cabinets or hard drives, and most of the material within them never leaves the project offices. For managing bibliographic data, editing projects may rely on a variety of reference management systems throughout their decades of existence. These systems include various combinations of physical filing cabinets, library-cataloguing software, custom applications built on relational databases, and specialized reference management software such as Zotero or EndNote. To varying degrees, these systems have allowed the projects to organize and manage descriptions of the sources they consult.

In addition to their notes, references, clippings, and photocopies, editorial projects also rely on specialized and locally developed tools for recording structured compilations of data such as itineraries, chronologies, and legislative histories. Editors of personal papers usually need to create a detailed itinerary of their subjects' movements. The MSPP and ECSSBAP keep these types of records in Microsoft Access and dBase III databases, respectively. Researchers at the EGP keep detailed records of Emma Goldman's lecture tours[4] and have made chronologies inside Microsoft Word and Word Perfect files for events such as the assassination of President William McKinley, the Preparedness Day Bombing of 1916, and the rise of the Industrial Workers of the World. Similarly, editors might create uniquely detailed legislative and legal histories of specific topics as the ECSSBAP editors have. Additionally, there are hundreds of informal chronologies spread across the working notes of each project.

Some technologically sophisticated projects also maintain specialized and locally developed tools for managing names (Hajo 1991). Names are always a challenge for historical research, and this is especially true for editorial projects. For example, many of the women researched by the MSPP had multiple different married names and alternated between using their maiden name and their married name at a given time. Dorothy Hamilton Brush, a close friend of Sanger's, appears in documents variously as Dorothy Adams Hamilton, Dorothy Brush, Dorothy Dick, and Dorothy Wamsley. Chinese and Indian names appearing in English-language documents may be transliterated in a wide variety of ways. Nicknames and children who share names with their parents or grandparents are also sources of confusion. A name authority database records preferred names, variant names, and identifying codes for every individual researched by the project. Each primary and secondary document controlled by the project is examined for personal names, and each name found is searched for in the name authority database. If a matching individual is found, the document is tagged

4 Some of which have been published as linked data at http://metadata.berkeley.edu/emma/. Accessed on 23 December 2014.

with an identifying code for that individual, and if the form of the name found in the document is a new variant, it is added to the name authority database. If no match is found, a new authority is created. To verify spelling and usage, periodically the name authority database will be manually checked against external authority files such as the Library of Congress Name Authority file.

Problems with current tools

The tools described above generally enable an editorial project to meet its goal of publishing edited volumes (though these often appear well behind schedule). But the organization and management of the valuable working notes these projects produce leaves much to be desired. While reference-management software usually provides some means of adding notes to individual entries, this functionality is insufficient to capture the cross-referencing that ties together the threads running through consulted sources. So working notes have tended to live separate lives from bibliographic descriptions, and as a result, notes on a particular source or topic may spread across handwritten notes, annotated photocopies, and word processing files. Consequently, duplication and loss of content is rampant. It is a major challenge to enable fine-grained access to and indexing of notes without making researchers feel as if they are working with "a million little pieces". On the one hand, researchers ought to be able to search for and link to "atomic" notes taken on a single source document as it relates to one narrow topic. Yet they also need to be able to work with flexible aggregations of these small 'atoms' in ways that feel natural to them.

One of the ways researchers would like to work with their notes is through visualization. Editors often wish to create visualizations displaying temporal, geospatial, or collective biographical information to concisely express large datasets, reinforce explanations, or offer aesthetically pleasing displays for public exhibition. But the difficulty of aggregating and repurposing the information in their working notes often precludes this. Working notes stored in formats such as WordPerfect documents require non-trivial amounts of special post-processing in order to turn them into structured data that can then be fed to visualization libraries. This requires outsourcing such work to experts who have mastered the use of specialized tools for text processing and data visualization, thereby decoupling the visualization of information from the process of research that created it. This becomes a problem if, for example, a researcher who is a technological layperson wants to correct or amend a timeline created by a since-departed specialist. The problem is not a lack of tools for generating map displays, timelines, prosopographies, and the like, but, rather, how to incorporate such tools into the work routines of hard-pressed editors and their assistants with an acceptably low threshold of learning and effort.

Finally, just as the research of individual editorial projects is unnecessarily fragmented across different working notes due to organizational issues, the funding and organization of editorial projects leads to unnecessary fragmentation of research across different projects and over time. The majority of the research produced by editorial projects is not included in the published volumes, is not shared with other researchers, and is discarded when grants for publication expire. Editors can and do ask editors elsewhere for help on specific topics, but answering may be time-consuming and they do not want to burden overworked colleagues with repeated requests for help. This results in fragmentation across parallel but related research efforts. Another kind of fragmentation occurs over time. Scholarly editing requires a sustained investment of highly specialized expertise, but long-term funding is difficult to find and usually narrowly limited to support for the eventual published edition. When the manuscript of the final volume is ready for publication, the editors and staff retire or move on and their working notes become effectively inaccessible if not discarded. But even as projects expire, scholarship continues. The ideal would be if the editorial "workshop" could remain ready to support resumed scholarship as and when labor and funding allow.

Editors' Notes

It is to address the problems discussed above that we have developed Editors' Notes,[5] an open-source hosted service for organizing the research of documentary editing projects (Figure 4.2, p. 54). Editors' Notes enables the publishing, sharing, and editing of working notes throughout the research process, from the initial posing of specific research questions all the way through to the authoring of polished footnotes and articles. The mission of the service is much the same as the one William Thoms (1849, 2) identified when he founded *Notes and Queries*: to provide a "medium by which much valuable information may become a sort of common property among those who can appreciate and use it".

Editors' Notes is organized around *notes*, *documents*, and *topics* (Figure 4.3, p. 54). A note is any kind of working note written by an editor. Editors can use a WYSIWYG interface to easily edit notes, and all past versions of edited notes are

5 http://editorsnotes.org/. Accessed on 23 December 2014.

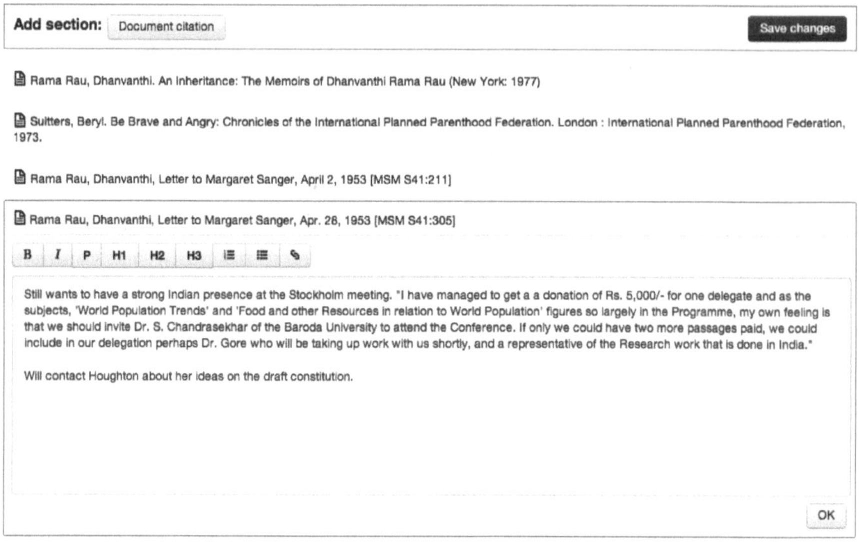

Figure 4.2: Using Editors' Notes to edit one section of a working note on 'Dhanvanthi Rama Rau & the Fourth International Conference on Planned Parenthood'.

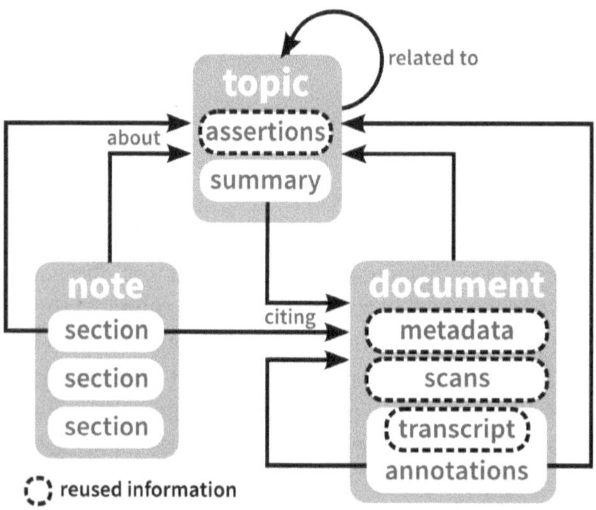

Figure 4.3: Part of the Editors' Notes data model. Factual assertions, metadata, scans and transcripts may be authored locally or linked to elsewhere.

saved. Notes are stored as HTML, so they may have hyperlinks and all the other features that HTML enables. Notes are structured into topic-specific and source-specific sections, allowing researchers to search for and link to note sections taken on a single source document as it relates to one narrow topic. For example, a working note on "Dhanvanthi Rama Rau & the Fourth International Conference on Planned Parenthood" (Figure 4.2) might reference dozens of documents and relate to other topics such as the Family Planning Association of India. Researchers can work with these note sections in the context of the broader working note, or they can pull together all the note sections about Rama Rau, whether or not these were taken in the course of researching "Dhanvanthi Rama Rau & the Fourth International Conference on Planned Parenthood". Each note is categorized based on its completeness: notes are open when they require more work; closed when deemed completed; and hibernating when a resolution remains desired but appears impractical, of low priority, or unobtainable given available sources.

Notes cite or explain documents. A document is anything that an editor is editing (e.g. the letters, diary entries, speeches, etc. that are the focus of the project) or is citing (any supporting evidence found in the course of the editor's research). Documents may have attached scans, transcripts (with optional annotations), and hyperlinks to external websites. Transcripts can be footnoted, and footnotes can cite other documents. Editors' Notes integrates with Zotero to manage document metadata (e.g. item type, author, title, archive), enabling the input and output of documents as structured bibliographic records (Shaw, Golden and Buckland 2012).

Notes and documents are indexed using terms drawn from a controlled vocabulary of topics. Topics may be person names, organization names, place names, event names, publication names, or names of concepts or themes. Each topic may have a summary, a free-form textual description or explanation of the topic. We can think of topics as subject authority records, with support for variant spellings, aliases, etc., but they can go beyond that, with support for various kinds of relations among topics, e.g. personal relations between persons, involvement of persons and organizations in events, and so on.

Integrating linked data into Editors' Notes

The topics in Editors' Notes provide a natural point for integration with and consumption of linked data from libraries and other cultural heritage institutions. Topics can be augmented with structured assertions created locally and/or imported from trusted external datasets. These assertions can then be used as the basis for specialized search and visualization interfaces. Assertions may relate separate topics, and just as topics are used to index notes and documents, relationships between topics might also be used for indexing and discovery. For example, Emma Goldman and Alexander Berkman were not only lovers but also co-editors of the anarchist journal *Mother Earth*. Their co-editing relationship might be used to index a document that is relevant to the latter relationship but not the former.

To investigate these possibilities, we added to Editors' Notes capabilities for harvesting and editing linked data (Shaw and Buckland 2011). The harvester ran periodically, looking for new linked data related to topics. For each topic name, the harvester queried a co-reference service (Glaser, Jaffri and Millard 2009) to obtain sets of candidate URIs for that name. Each set contained URIs that had been asserted to refer to the same entity. For example, when queried with the name "Emma Goldman", the first set of URIs returned by the co-reference service includes the identifiers for Emma Goldman from VIAF (Loesch 2011) and Freebase (Bollacker et al. 2008). For each set in the response, each URI in the set was dereferenced and the resulting data was examined. If, for any of the dereferenced URIs, this data included a valid label, and the value of this label matched the topic name, then the whole set of candidate URIs was accepted. Otherwise, the set was rejected and the next set was examined. In this way, the harvester obtained a set of zero or more URIs for each topic. The harvester then stored all assertions obtained by dereferencing the URIs.

Editorial control over assertions about topics

Each assertion was stored in two separate graphs: one graph contained all the candidate assertions about a given topic, while the other contained all the assertions from the same source (e.g. DBpedia, VIAF, Deutsche Nationalbibliothek, etc.). The topic-specific graphs made it simple to display all the assertions found for a given topic, while the source-specific graphs made it easy to request fresh data from a given source.

Once a set of candidate assertions about a topic had been obtained, editors could use the linked data editor to accept or reject them (see Figure 4.4, p. 57). Accepting and rejecting assertions could happen at different levels of specificity. An editor could reject a single assertion that she judged to be inaccurate. Or she could choose to reject all assertions that shared a given predicate that had been judged irrelevant to the editing project. For example, many DBpedia (Auer et al. 2007) resources contain assertions about what templates are used on their corresponding Wikipedia pages, and this information is not likely to interest editors.

Finally, an editor could accept all the assertions about a given topic, or all the assertions from a given source. When an editor accepted assertions from a given source, this was treated as evidence that the identifier from that source referred to the same entity, and an owl:sameAs assertion was created linking the topic to that identifier. Thus the process of accepting assertions had the effect of linking Editors' Notes topics to standard identifiers in external systems. Accepted assertions were inserted into a graph associated with the editor who accepted them. This way the provenance of published assertions was made clear, and editors could choose whether they needed to further assess assertions accepted by less expert contributors (i.e. student assistants).

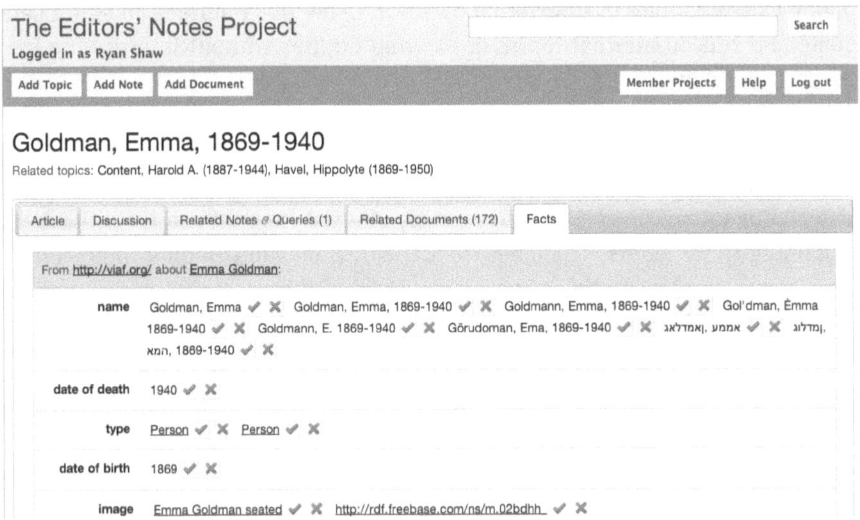

Figure 4.4: The interface for accepting or rejecting assertions in the first iteration of the Editors' Notes linked data editor.

Lessons learned and current direction

Our pilot project demonstrated that it was possible to automatically harvest relevant linked data from cultural-heritage institutions and other datasets. A simple interface for accepting or rejecting harvested assertions made it easy for researchers to exert editorial control over the harvested data. Ultimately, however, our pilot did not demonstrate that the benefits of additional structured data were worth editors spending their (or their interns') time accepting or rejecting it. Thus our current development effort is focused on not simply aggregating and editing linked data but usefully exploiting it to researchers' benefit. Before turning to a discussion of those expected benefits, we will briefly describe the new tools we are currently developing and how they exploit linked data.

The first change involves how topics are created and linked to. In the pilot implementation, editors created topics to label and index their notes and documents, and these topics were later reconciled to external identifiers in a separate batch process. In the new system, editors fluidly create, link to, and reconcile topics within the note-taking process. When in the course of note-taking an editor types the name of a place, person, organization, or other such entity, the interface offers elective autocompletion from a ranked list of matching candidates found among existing topics or in external datasets. Using this interface an editor can create and link to internal topics or external entities without interrupting her research workflow.

For example, suppose an editor is creating a note about Rama Rau's role in planning the Fourth ICPP in Stockholm, Sweden. After she types the letters "R-a-m-a R-a-u" she presses the tab key, triggering a search of the Editors' Notes entity index for existing topics or previously indexed external entities with labels containing those letters. The label "Rama Rau, Dhanvanti Handoo, 1893–1987" appears in a small menu below the cursor, and the editor presses enter to confirm that this is the Rama Rau referred to in the note. Because this label is from an external entity not previously used within the site, it is automatically established as a new Editors' Notes topic. The text of the note is left unchanged, but a link is created between the string "Rama Rau" in the note text and the new topic.

In case no suitable internal topics exist and none of the previously indexed external entities are relevant, the system will enable incremental creation and "offline" asynchronous reconciliation of new topics. For example, suppose the editor types the letters "S-t-o-c-k-h-o-l-m" and presses the tab key, again triggering an entity search. This time no suitable results are found, so instead of candidate labels, a small "Create Topic?" menu appears with the options Person, Place, Organization, Event, and (selected by default) Topic. The editor selects "Place" and is prompted to edit the default topic label "Stockholm". She adds "Sweden" to complete the topic label, and a link is created between the mention of "Stockholm" in the text of the note and the newly-created topic labelled "Stockholm, Sweden". The editor then continues with her research and note-taking.

In the background, Editors' Notes has begun querying a configurable set of linked data endpoints, trying to reconcile the label Stockholm, Sweden with identifiers managed by those endpoints. It discovers the following candidate identifiers:[6]

6 All URLs given in the text were accessed on 24 December 2014.

- http://viaf.org/viaf/153530943 (VIAF geographic name Stockholm (Sweden));
- http://sws.geonames.org/2673730 (Geonames place Stockholm), and
- http://dbpedia.org/resource/Stockholm (DBpedia populated place entity Stockholm).

Once this search for candidate identifiers has finished, an unobtrusive notification appears, letting the editor know that she can finish the reconciliation process when she wishes. Not wanting to interrupt her work, the editor ignores the notification.

The next day, the editor logs into Editors' Notes again. On her dashboard she sees a reminder that the new topic "Stockholm" has not yet been reconciled. She clicks on the reminder and is taken to a page displaying data from VIAF, Geonames, and DBpedia. Scanning the data, she sees that the entities identified within each of these services are equivalent to one another.[7] She decides that they are also equivalent to the Editors' Notes Topic "Stockholm, Sweden" and clicks a button to finish the reconciliation process, thereby associating the three external identifiers with the new topic.

Our pilot implementation enabled storing and editing assertions about topics from external datasets, but provided no incentive for editors to do this. In the new system, storing and editing external assertions about topics happens in the context of sorting and filtering lists of notes and documents and creating simple visualizations of the information held in working notes. Thus aggregating and editing linked data is not an unmotivated activity, but is seamlessly integrated into the process of managing and using working notes. Thus through a combination of selectively importing data from external links and entering it locally, topics are gradually and incrementally enriched from a mere list of generic "things" to a structured group of semantically distinct and descriptive entities suitable for advanced querying and manipulation. Importantly, researchers have full editorial control over this data, ensuring its high quality and compatibility with their painstaking scholarship. In addition to editing linked data associated with topics, editors also can create notes consisting of structured data rather than free text. This is expected to be useful for creating highly structured working notes such as itineraries, chronologies, and legislative histories.

Many interactions with Editors' Notes involve working with lists of note sections and documents:

1. Upon browsing to the topic "India, birth control movement in", one sees lists of note sections and documents related to that topic (Figure 4.5, p. 60).

7 This may be asserted by an external linking framework such as Silk (Volz et al. 2009).

2. The note on "Dhanvanthi Rama Rau & the Fourth International Conference on Planned Parenthood" is a list of note sections on various letters and reports that reference that event (Figure 4.1).
3. A search for "Rama Rau" returns a list of notes and documents with that name in their text (Figure 4.6, p. 61).

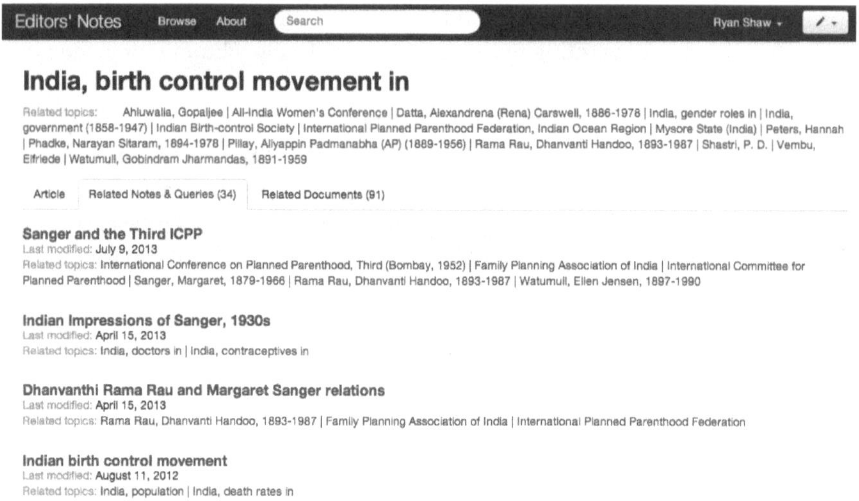

Figure 4.5: Notes and documents related to the topic "India, birth control movement in".

Working flexibly with lists like these requires the ability to filter and sort them easily. Currently researchers can filter and sort lists of documents (and the notes that cite them) using the bibliographic metadata associated with the documents. But when not only documents, but also places, people, organizations, and events have structured data associated with them, we can provide far more powerful facilities for filtering and sorting notes and documents. Given a list of notes on "India, birth control movement in", users can filter and sort them not only using the dates of the cited documents (as they currently can), but also using the locations and birth and death dates of the people referenced in the notes, the locations and dates of existence of the organizations referenced, or the locations and dates of the events referenced.

Furthermore, by taking advantage of structured spatial and temporal metadata, we are no longer restricted to presenting lists of notes and documents textually. The note on "Dhanvanthi Rama Rau & the Fourth International Conference on Planned Parenthood" can become viewable not only as a text document, but also as a map of specific locations in Stockholm and Bombay, a timeline of dates

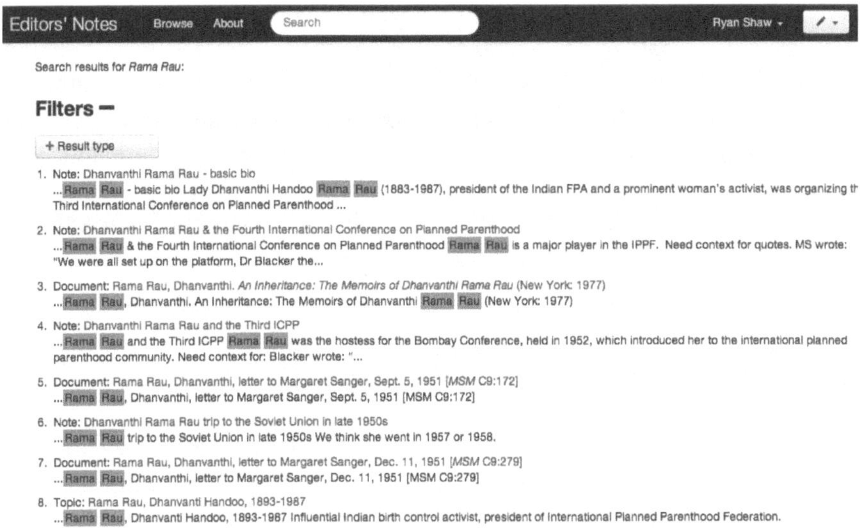

Figure 4.6: A search for documents with the string "Rama Rau" in their text.

associated with the conference, or a network of relationships among people and organizations. Maps, timelines, and network graphs correspond most naturally to places, events, and personal relationships, but any topic which has geographic coordinates can be mapped, any topic with time points or ranges can be put on a timeline, and any relationships among topics can be visualized as a network. These three genres of visualization together are, therefore, broadly applicable to any kind of structured data about topics that might be gathered. Documents have equivalent data (when and where published; authorship) allowing the same types of visualizations for them too. So, for example, a map display can show any location(s) mentioned in a note, with options to display the locations of other related topics and documents in any number of ways as determined by the interests of the editors.

Now, instead of doing unmotivated data wrangling, editors can do it gradually and incrementally as part of the process of sorting, filtering, and visualizing their working notes. For example, suppose an editor decides she wants to visualize the network of people involved with the International Planned Parenthood Federation (IPPF). She generates an initial visualization by importing assertions from Wikipedia to show a network of relations among people involved with the IPPF including Margaret Sanger, Dhanvanthi Rama Rau, Margaret Pyke, and Lloyd Morain. But the visualization is missing labels for the links between these people and the IPPF, since that information is not provided in Wikipedia. She clicks on the node for "Pyke, Margaret Chubb, 1893–1966" in the visualization and is shown all the structured data associated with that topic, including Pyke's birthdate, birthplace, date of death, and place of death. She presses the edit button and is presented with an editable tabular view of the facts. She edits the assertion linking Pyke to the IPPF to reflect that she was head of the Family Planning Association of England, a national affiliate of the IPPF. Although this information was added to the "Pyke, Margaret Chubb, 1893–1966" topic, it will now also appear among the facts related to the "International Planned Parenthood Federation" topic.

Benefits of consuming linked data

The tools described can potentially remove some tedious, duplicative work from everyday research. Editors can import contextual details of, for example, persons (e.g. birth and death dates, place of birth, and other names) or of places (alternative names, containing jurisdiction, latitude and longitude) without researching or transcribing these details at every mention. Data accumulation is incremental and comes as a by-product of the routine editing effort. Linking to external datasets can bring the benefit of automatic updating as additions and corrections are made to the resources to which they are linked. These are welcome conveniences. But the major potential benefits of consuming linked data are threefold: making working notes repurposable, replacing name authority files with naming services, and shifting the focus of editorial projects from product to process.

Making working notes repurposable

Researchers already spend considerable time and effort producing working notes. But because these notes consist primarily of unstructured text, they are not easily repurposable. More structured and therefore repurposable working notes enable researchers to use their research in new ways. For example, a researcher can aggregate the chronologies of several different events together into a larger timeline to look for connections or patterns that might not have been evident when viewing each separately. Reducing the expertise required to create such visualizations enables and encourages experimentation with the different kinds of information held in working notes. Giving researchers without specialized knowledge the ability to author, edit, and control structured documents and derived visualizations has the potential to change the nature of how researchers use their working notes. Instead of visualizations like maps and timelines being handcrafted for one-off exhibitions, they become works in progress, able to be controlled with the same editorial touch as the textual record.

Replacing name authority files with naming services

Linking names to external authorities enables project-specific name authority databases to be replaced or augmented by shared naming and reconciliation services, which has a number of advantages. The process of checking spelling and usage can be further automated, and every project benefits whenever the naming service is updated. A naming service can power an auto-completion function that allows editors to quickly and easily link names to identifiers in any context, such as authoring a working note. And rather than using the separate name authority database to produce reports of variant names to be manually consulted when searching, a naming service can be used to automatically expand searches to include variant names. Finally, all of these amenities can be extended beyond personal names to other kinds of names (events, organizations, places, subjects). Another benefit is that by mapping their topics and entities to identifiers for those topics and entities elsewhere, editorial projects can make their research products more widely accessible. By linking their working notes to external identifiers for people, places, organizations, events and ideas, editorial projects make their work far more interoperable with other scholarly projects, library catalogues, archival finding aids, and open knowledge projects such as Wikipedia.

Shifting from product to process

Used shrewdly, the web and linked data have the potential to dissolve the silos that isolate research in separate editing projects and to enable the serendipitous discovery of useful material by other researchers and the wider public. They also have the potential to shift the focus of editorial project funding and organization away from the published edition as the one and only product. Currently editorial expertise and project working resources are treated as expendable means to that sole objective. But changed technology makes it imaginable to reverse that relationship. In this view the editorial "workshop" (expertise and working notes) could be enduring assets and the published editions would become intermittent and valued by-products. Scholarly communication could be greatly extended if it were feasible not only for researchers anywhere to have sustained access to the working notes, but also for researchers anywhere to add supplementary notes, corrections and additions to them (with clearly separate attribution) in the future as and when interest, ability, and resources allow.

Conclusion

Documentary editing projects exemplify a form of library and archives-based research that partially replicates the organizational infrastructure of libraries, archives, and special collections. Were that infrastructure to be made usable in a standardized form such as linked data, these projects could both re-use data from and contribute data back to catalogues, finding aids, and other sources. These tools would no longer be used solely to find documents but would contribute to the ongoing organization of research that uses and expands upon those documents. Ideally, the result would be a continuously updated compilation of facts related to specific people, places, organizations, events and ideas.

For this vision to become reality, it will be necessary to find ways of consuming and using linked data that accord with the working practices of researchers. User interfaces for consuming independently originated linked data must save users more time and effort than they require. Achieving this ideal will require close attention to specific use cases and contexts. Linked data tools and infrastructure must adapt to these use cases and contexts, rather than vice versa. It remains to be seen whether this challenge can be met by the linked data research community, which has tended to put the cart before the horse by focusing on the technical details of data formats and communication protocols instead of trying to understand potential contexts of use.

Acknowledgements

We are grateful to the Andrew W. Mellon Foundation for funding "Editorial Practices and the Web" (http://ecai.org/mellon2010) and for the cooperation and feedback of our colleagues at the Emma Goldman Papers, the Margaret Sanger Papers, the Elizabeth Cady Stanton and Susan B. Anthony Papers, and the Joseph A. Labadie Collection.

References

Auer, Sören, Christian Bizer, Georgi Kobilarov, Jens Lehmann, Richard Cyganiak and Zachary Ives. 2007. "Dbpedia: a nucleus for a web of open data." In *The Semantic Web: 6th International Semantic Web Conference, 2nd Asian Semantic Web Conference, ISWC 2007 + ASWC 2007, Busan, Korea, November 11–15, 2007, Proceedings*, edited by K Aberer et al., 722–735. Berlin: Springer.

Bollacker, Kurt D., Colin Evans, Praveen Paritosh, Tim Sturge and Jamie Taylor. 2008. "Freebase: a collaboratively created graph database for structuring human knowledge" *Proceedings of the 2008 ACM SIGMOD International Conference on Management of Data – SIGMOD '08*. doi:10.1145/1376616.1376746. Accessed on 23 December 2014.

Glaser, Hugh, Afraz Jaffri and Ian C. Millard. 2009. "Managing co-reference on the Semantic Web" *Proceedings of the WWW2009 Workshop on linked data on the Web*. http://ceur-ws.org/Vol-538/ldow2009_paper11.pdf. Accessed on 23 December 2014.

Hajo, Cathy Moran. 1991. "Computerizing control over authority names at the Margaret Sanger Papers" *Documentary Editing* 13(2): 35–39.

Kline, Mary-Jo and Susan Holbrook Perdue. 2008. *A Guide to Documentary Editing*. 3rd edition. Charlottesville: University of Virginia Press.

Loesch, Martha Fallahay. 2011. "VIAF (The Virtual International Authority File) – http://viaf.org" *Technical Services Quarterly* 28(2): 255–256. doi:10.1080/07317131.2011.546304. Accessed on 23 December 2014.

Rutner, Jennifer and Roger C. Schonfeld. 2012. *Supporting the Changing Research Practices of Historians*. New York: Ithaka S+R. http://www.sr.ithaka.org/sites/default/files/reports/supporting-the-changing-research-practices-of-historians.pdf. Accessed on 23 December 2014.

Shaw, Ryan and Michael Buckland. 2011. "Editorial control over linked data" *Proceedings of the American Society for Information Science and Technology* 48(1): 1–4. doi:10.1002/meet.2011.14504801296. Accessed on 23 December 2014.

Shaw, Ryan, Patrick Golden and Michael Buckland. 2012. "Integrating collaborative bibliography and research" *Proceedings of the American Society for Information Science and Technology* 49(1): 1–4. doi:10.1002/meet.14504901245. Accessed on 23 December 2014.

Thoms, W. J. 1849. "Notes and queries" *Notes and Queries*, 1st series 1(1): 1–3. doi:10.1093/nq/s1-I.1.1. Accessed on 23 December 2014.

Volz, Julius, Christian Bizer, Martin Gaedkeand Georgi Kobilarov. 2009. "Silk—a link discovery framework for the web of data" *Proceedings of the 2nd Workshop about linked data on the Web (LDOW2009), Madrid.*. http://ceur-ws.org/Vol-538/ldow2009_paper13.pdf. Accessed on 24 December 2014.

Timm Heuss, Bernhard Humm, Tilman Deuschel, Torsten Fröhlich, Thomas Herth and Oliver Mitesser

5 Semantically Guided, Situation-Aware Literature Research

Abstract: Searching literature in bibliographic portals is often a trial-and-error process, consisting of manually and repeatedly firing search requests. This paper presents an automatic guidance system that supports users in their literature research with a stepwise refinement process, based on their needs. Algorithms operate on various different data sets, including valuable world knowledge in form of Linked Open Data, which is streamlined and indexed by a semantic extraction, transform and load process. Search results are composed dynamically and are visualized in an innovative way as a topic wheel. In this paper, we describe the prototype of this system and our current work in progress, including first user evaluations.

Keywords: Linked Open Data, Semantic information visualization, Library guide and search system, Information Retrieval, HTML5

Introduction

In 2009, Tim Berners-Lee introduced linked open data (LOD) as a paradigm to exchange data in order to allow others to re-use and to refer to this data without barriers (Berners-Lee 2009). Since then, many governments[1] and organizations[2] have understood the LOD-vision as a public service providing a new level of transparency and launched portals that offer most different data sets in LOD, to anyone who is interested.

Publishing data that everybody can use is a great benefit for a citizen. However, pure availability does not necessarily lead to new and exciting applications. In fact, advanced engineering and domain-specific skills are required to build applications that benefit from LOD.

In the project Mediaplatform, we are researching new and enhanced ways of searching and displaying media stocks, for example books in a library. Thereby,

1 A famous LOD government portal is, for example, the British data.gov.uk. Accessed on 27 December 2014.

2 For example, the Project Gutenberg dataset, http://datahub.io/dataset/fu-berlin-project-gutenberg. Accessed on 27 December 2014.

we observed that a classic book search is often a trial-and-error process, consisting of firing a search request, receiving either too many or too few results and then manually finding a suitable refinement or generalization of the search terms. We think that, today, there is a chance to perform literature research much more intelligently.

Compare the above-mentioned trial-and-error process with the way well informed human librarians recommend suitable literature to a customer. Librarians would usually not wait for customers to refine their book requests. Instead, they would rather ask questions in order to get a better understanding of the customers' needs, make preselections and recommendations. Customers often only roughly describe what they are looking for. With the competent help of librarians, they will find the intended literature – or other alternatives that meet the requirements much better. There would be no trial and error but a systematically guided, stepwise refinement process.

To pursuit the vision of this human-like guidance, we develop an application that supports library users semantically in their literature research, i.e., based on the understanding of their search inputs. It has to cope with different situations, if there are either no, too many or too few results.

The remainder of this paper is organized as follows. First, we define the different challenges such an application is faced with. Next, we first clarify the role of LOD, and then we introduce the application's logical components. Then we successively present technical insights. evaluate the approach, present related work and conclude the paper, outlining future work.

Problem statement

The goal of this work is to enable semantically guided, situation-aware literature research via an application. The requirements are as follows:

1. Literature research: It shall be possible to find and retrieve literature, e.g., books, articles, or monographs, which are relevant[3] to the user. Users may be students or researchers.
2. Semantically guided: The application shall assist users to find relevant literature,[4] i.e., by guiding the users. The guidance shall be based on knowledge about the users' interests and about the semantic content of the literature.

3 A first survey we conducted showed that relevant information for making a decision which book to borrow is the table of contents, description and title.

4 The survey showed that users know what they want to know before they start their search, but that it is more difficult to find appropriate keywords.

Users shall have the impression that the application understands them similarly to human librarians. The guidance shall be goal-oriented, i.e., guide the user as quickly as possible to relevant literature.
3. Situation-aware: The application shall be aware of the situation of the user and of the retrieval process and adapt the guidance strategy accordingly. For example, if the user provides a general search term with too many search results, the application suggests sensible specializations. On the other hand, if the search terms are too specific to find any research result, the application suggests related terms.
4. Intuitive: Users shall be able to use the application without training or studying a user manual.
5. Device-independent: The application shall be useable on all state-of-the-art devices, i.e., mobile phones, tablet computers, and personal computers including touch and pointer interaction, even at the same time.
6. Good performance: The application shall allow users to work in their own pace in a pleasant way. In particular, response times shall be below 1 sec. for common use cases.

An Application for semantically guided, situation-aware literature research

The Role of LOD

The concept of Linked Open Data (LOD) is most important for the success of endeavours like the one described here. This is for the following reasons:
1. Large communities formalize knowledge in very large data sets, which would be impossible for individual development projects. This includes quality assurance and permanently keeping the data sets up to date.
2. Standardized formats allow processing the data sets.
3. The free use of the data sets is ensured by appropriate licences.

However, there are major challenges in using such data sets in applications as described here. Bowker and Star (1999, 131) correctly state: “Classifications that appear natural, eloquent, and homogeneous within a given human context appear forced and heterogeneous outside of that context”. This may result in the following problems:

1. Structure and content of the data sets only partially match the requirements of an application. Take, for example, an application that needs to provide the epoch in which an artist worked, e.g., Michelangelo worked in the epoch Renaissance. The YAGO ontology (Suchanek, Kasneci and Weikum 2007) contains this information, but not explicitly via a property "epoch" but implicitly via the property "rdf:type" with the value "wikicategory_Rennaissance_artists". This is also a key problem when implementing a search mechanism across different vocabularies (Schreiber et al. 2008).
2. Structure and content of different data sets to be integrated are only partially compatible. For example, in medicine ontologies like the NCI thesaurus (Golbeck et al. 2003), concepts are modelled as OWL classes and the relation with broader concepts are modelled via "rdfs:subclassOf". Other ontologies model concepts as instances and the relation with broader concepts explicitly via "skos:broader" [SKOS]. There are no uniform queries over such ontologies when they are simply merged.
3. The structure of data sets does not allow efficient query access in certain situations. For example, Heuss (2013, 4) describes a conceptually simple query to the SPARQL endpoint of DBpedia which was rejected with error message: "The estimated execution time 7219 (sec) exceeds the limit of 3000 (sec)" – the reason being that the structure of DBpedia is not optimized for this kind of query.

To leverage the advantages of LOD while coping with the problems described, we utilize a "Semantic Extraction, Transformation, and Loading (Semantic ETL)" approach.

Semantic ETL

Semantic ETL consists of the steps (1) *extraction*, (2) *transformation / semantic enrichment*, and (3) *loading*.

Extraction

In the first step, data sources are acquired which have the following characteristics:
1. *Relevant*: The data sources must contain information which is relevant for the respective use cases, here semantically guided literature research. For example, the GND[5] data set of the German National Library contains a tax-

5 http://www.dnb.de/DE/Standardisierung/GND/gnd_node.html. Accessed on 27 December 2014.

onomy of subject terms which allows finding broader and narrower terms for a given term.
2. *Sufficient quality*: The information contained in the data sources must be of sufficient quality. For example, GND has been manually edited and quality-controlled by experts over a period of several decades.
3. *Structured*: The information is provided in a structured, machine-processable way. For example, GND is provided in RDF. Any other structured, documented format like, e.g., Pica+[6] is suitable, too.
4. *Accessible*: GND is accessible as Linked Open Data. However, commercially available data sources are suitable, too.

The careful selection of suitable data sources is a design-time step to be performed by human experts. During execution time, the extracted data sources are stored in a staging area.

Transformation and semantic enrichment

In the second step, the data sources are pre-processed, including the following sub-steps.
1. *Format transformation*: In this step, the formats of the different data sources are transformed into a common, structured data format, e.g., into JSON notation.[7] Source formats are XML dialects, RDF, CSV, etc.
2. *Semantic enrichment*: In this step, heuristics are used in order to deduce additional information from the data sources. For example, subject terms in GND lack a ranking with respect to their relevance. So, the term "Java <Programming language>" has numerous narrower terms, including more relevant ones like "Java Enterprise Edition" and less relevant ones like "Visual J++". With the heuristic that the relevance of a term increases with the number of publications with this term as subject, a term ranking can be derived from the publication stock. More complex semantic enrichment necessitates the matching and merging of corresponding entities from different data sources via heuristic methods.
3. *Performance tuning*: In some cases, it is advantageous to denormalize data and to influence the indexing process for high-performance access.

---

6 German description of data format http://www.gbv.de/wikis/cls/PICA-Format. Accessed on 27 December 2014.

7 http://www.json.org/. Accessed on 27 December 2014.

Loading

In the last step, the transformed and semantically enriched data is loaded into a data store. The data store must provide the following characteristics:

1. *Sufficient query functionality*: e.g., it should be possible to query for literature which has a given term as subject, including narrower terms, ignoring case, and allowing for phonological ambiguities (e.g., "Meyer" versus "Maier").
2. *Sufficient performance*: The data store must allow for high-performance access to large data sets.

Retrieval

The Retrieval component delegates incoming search queries to the involved data stores, which have been previously filled by the Semantic ETL process. There are three stores:

1. *The DocumentStore* contains metadata about the media entities, for example books.
2. *The AuthorStore* contains metadata for persons that are connected to the media entities in the DocumentStore. For books, this connection is usually an authorship.
3. *The TermStore* contains general purpose, cross-domain technical terms and their senses, stored in a hierarchical structure. Thus, for a book, not only its respective category can be found as an entry, but also broader or narrower categories.

The following two sections describe a typical search scenario and how the different stores are involved. Store results are never directly returned to the user, they are just collected as evaluation input for the next component, the Guiding Agent.

AuthorStore and DocumentStore search capabilities

A typical search query that involves the AuthorStore as well as the DocumentStore might be the query "Russel Norvig Artifical Intelligence". After this query is delegated by the Retrieval component, the DocumentStore returns, among others, "Artifical Intelligence – A Modern Approach" and the AuthorStore the corresponding authors "Stuart Russel" and "Peter Norvig".

TermStore search capabilities

For the TermStore, a typical input might be the single word "Java". Thanks to the legwork done by Semantic ETL, the store finds three senses for "Java" – the island, the dance and the programming language – as well as broader and narrower concepts for each respective sense, e.g. "Object oriented programming languages" as broader concept of "Java" in the sense "Programming Language" or "Jakarta" as narrower concept of "Java" in the sense of "Island".

Guiding agent

The component providing the guiding logic follows an agent approach. For each user interaction step, it receives the current user action as input, and produces information for the user. Thereby, it performs the following steps: (1) *accept user input*; (2) *search data stores;* (3) *analyse situation / react accordingly*, and (4) *process and return result.*

Accept user input

The user can interact with the application in the following ways:

1. *Free text input*: The user may specify criteria in a text entry box for the literature research in natural language including, e.g., mentioning authors, subject terms, publication titles or parts thereof, publication dates, etc.
2. *Selected topics*: The user may select topics presented by the application in the previous interaction step.

Search data stores

The user input is utilized to retrieve relevant data from the data stores: AuthorStore, TermStore, and DocumentStore. The data store queries are generated depending on the user input as explained in the previous section.

Analyse situation and react accordingly

The agent analyses the retrieved data and uses heuristics to deal with different situations. Examples:

1. If the user input results in a large number of matching documents then the agent will guide the user to *refine* the request. To this end, topics are being generated that partition the result set.
2. If the user input results in no matching documents the agent will guide the user to *broaden* the request. To this end, topics are being generated that are related with the user request but will result in matching documents.

Process and return result

The agent's result returned to the user consists of a list of documents and a set of topics that may guide to the next step of literature research.

1. *Documents* are ranked according to the degree of matching the user input. Only sufficiently relevant documents are selected for the result – the remaining documents are filtered out.
2. *Topics* are generated using heuristics. For example, to refine a request, terms which are narrower than the terms specified by the user may be retrieved from the TermStore. Those narrower terms are considered relevant if they have relevant, matching documents. Such relevant terms can be prioritized and offered to the user as further topics.

Client

The application is a combination of a search-oriented system, providing books that are relevant to the user's request, and a browsing-oriented system, enhancing the search by the Guiding Agent's adaptive navigation support.

The adaptive interface is environment-aware and renders differently on different screen resolutions (Brusilovsky 2001). The client uses CSS media queries[8] to change layout and style for three different device classes: smartphone, tablet and desktop. A state machine determines which interactor shall be rendered. Thereby the application becomes faster on mobile devices by avoiding rendering all the interactors at first and hiding the interactors that are not required afterwards. The state machine also enables graceful degradation of interactors (Florins and Vanderdonckt 2004), based on different states. The guiding agent's visualization is rendered on a smartphone in landscape mode differently than on a smartphone in portrait mode, because the way users interact is different then, though the screen space stays the same (Nicolau and Jorge 2012).

8 http://www.w3.org/TR/css3-mediaqueries/. Accessed on 29 December 2014.

The Guiding Agent's visualization is inspired by Christopher Collins, who worked in the area of semantic information visualization research. The document content visualization DocuBurst is especially important for our work (Collins, Carpendale and Penn 2009).

DocuBurst visualises the content of documents by breaking it down to topics (Figure 5.1 left). These topics are represented in circular arcs, showing the superordinated topic in the center. The subordinated topics are ordered towards the edge.

Because the guiding agent's visualization looks like a wheel and can be spun, we call it the topic wheel. In contrast to DocuBurst, the topic wheel (Figure 5.1 right) is an interactor that does not visualise all the information available but enables the user on touch and non-touch interfaces to easily select recommended topics based on the current topic. Regarding desktop computers and convertibles, the user interface needs to satisfy touch and pointer input at the same time.

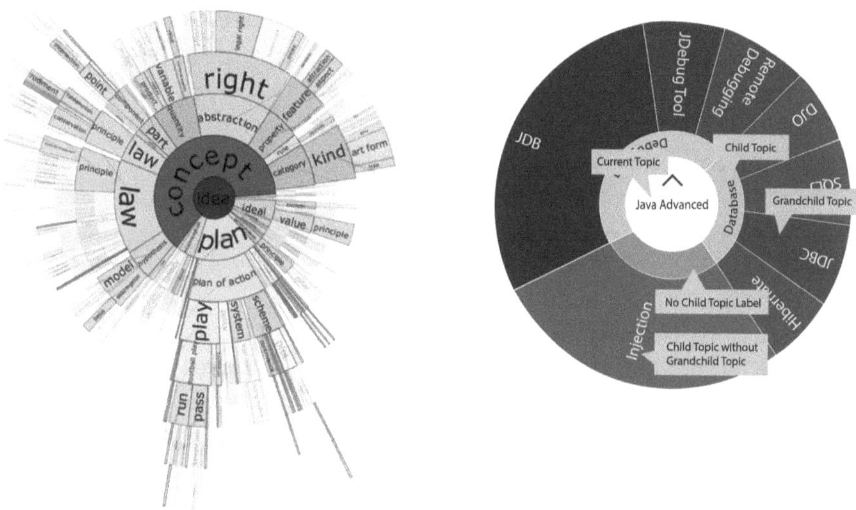

Figure 5.1: Left: DocuBurst visualization of a document by Christopher Collins. Right: Topic wheel, visualization of the content composed by the Guiding Agent.

The topics are ordered from centre to edge displaying a top-down hierarchy as in DocuBurst but showing only two degrees of relationship based on the current topic. Directly related topics are visualized as child topics between the centere and the edge. If a child topic has further subordinated topics, they are the grandchildren of the current topic and placed at the edge. The total number of child topics or grandchild topics is limited to 25. This way we can assure that the label of each topic inside the topic wheel is still readable and that the topic wheel does not become too complex for a user whose primary goal is a quick guidance in addition to the search-driven process.

The current topic is a search term, provided by the user. If there is no grandchild topic but only child topics, they are displayed as grandchild topics without a child topic label (Figure 5.1 right). This could be regarded as a logical inconsistency. However, early usability tests indicated that users understand the Guiding Agent better by visual consistency, i.e., by not having gaps in the circular visualization. Therefore, the child topic label is placed at the edge. This also solves the problem of lacking screen space if many child topics without grandchild topics are supposed to be rendered in the topic wheel.

The range of colour is based on the light spectrum from blue to red and finally violet. We place violet at the end, so the topic wheel will start with blue, followed by green, which creates more aesthetic visualizations as most users have a preference for blue and green (Deuschel and Vas 2012).

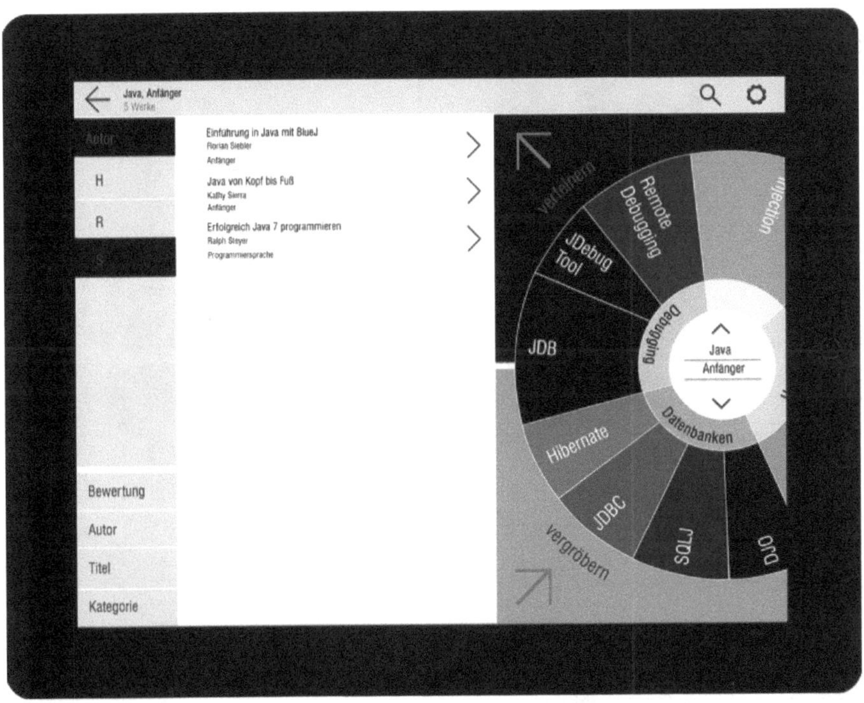

Figure 5.2: Adaptive interface of the application rendered for a tablet environment. The topic wheel is placed on the right.

Twenty-five shades of each colour represent a grandchild topic. Every shade has a brighter and less saturated version for the child topic. That way the topic wheel is able to display every scenario from one child topic and 25 grandchild topics and up to 25 child topics without grandchild topics. The topic wheel does not aim for complete representation of all available related topics, it displays the most relevant ones only (Figure 5.2). Therefore, it is necessary to sort them according to relevance.

Implementation

The Mediaplatform implementation is a client-server architecture, consisting of an HTML5 web app that communicates with an HTTP REST-based web service written in Java. Figure 5.3 depicts the involved layers and the corresponding components Guiding Agent, Retrieval and the Semantic ETL.

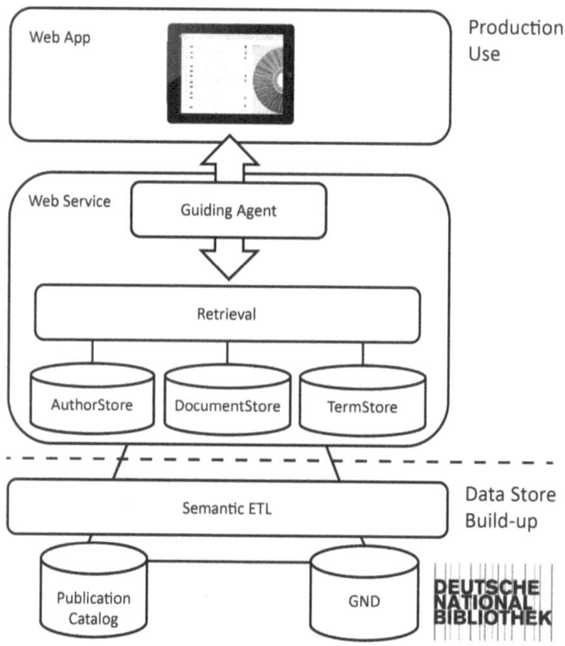

Figure 5.3: Architectural overview of the Mediaplatform, showing the components involved in the two modes "Data Store Build-up" and "Productional use".

The figure also shows that there are two main modes: (1) data store build up and (2) production use.

Data store build-up

As a preparatory step, the Semantic ETL component is executed to build up the AuthorStore, DocumentStore, and TermStore. It processes various kinds of inputs, including the GND data set of the German National Library[9] (RDF format) and the document stock of all libraries of the state of Hesse (Pica+ format).

As outlined above, the criteria for selecting the data-store technologies and products are (1) sufficient query functionality and (2) sufficient performance. For retrieving literature, fuzzy querying features such as case-insensitive search, allowing for phonological ambiguities, best guesses, support for lemma forms, and ratings are required. RDF-triple stores such as Virtuoso or OWLim do not provide such features. Such features are typically provided by search engines like Apache Lucene. Lucene also provides the necessary performance characteristics and has been chosen as the data-store technology.

The Semantic ETL process creates the stores as Lucene index structures. Lucene offers the suitable abstraction level to search engine interns but still gives the opportunity to manipulate delicate details, e.g., the exact kind of indexing of certain information. We use this to optimize the index structures towards the typical usage patterns of the Mediaplatform. For example, to create the contents of the topic wheel, the TermStore must find a given term with its corresponding broader and narrower concepts out of half a million records within a few ten milliseconds, as the subsequent Guiding Agent will conduct a time-consuming reasoning and optimization step prior to the final delivery to the client. The terms (subjects) in the input source GND, however, just refer to their respective broader terms, so the transitive relation to narrower terms is created during the Semantic ETL. It takes a few minutes to build up the index but in production, the transitive relations can then be accessed in about 20 milliseconds.

Production use

In production use, the Retrieval component fires queries on all three Lucene index structures, the AuthorStore, DocumentStore and the TermStore. The resulting entities from the stores are then processed in the Guiding Agent component, which conducts several heuristics, for example a prioritization or a preselection. We designed this reasoning of the Guiding Agent as an isolated step from the store queries, not just to have results from three stores as input for the reasoning,

---

9 http://www.dnb.de/DE/Standardisierung/GND/gnd_node.html. Accessed on 29 December 2014.

but also to incorporate statistics or to preview store results, and to take this valuable information in consideration, too.

On the client side, the data sets sent from the web service are displayed by an HTML5 web app. Due to the use of CSS media queries, it may be used on various devices, especially on mobile phones and tablets. We also use a number of common JavaScript frameworks, like jQuery mobile,[10] in order to respect the individual needs of the top three browsers Firefox, Chrome and Safari. We use Knockout[11] to implement a Model-View-ViewModel (MVVM) pattern and KineticJS[12] to build the canvas-based topic wheel which is rotated by CSS3 transitions.

Evaluation

In this section, we evaluate our approach with respect to the goals outlined in section "Problem Statement":

1. *Literature research*: The current prototype implementation allows users to find literature in the consolidated stock of all university libraries of the German state of Hesse including, overall, about 15 million publications.
2. *Semantically guided*: The guiding agent component implements logic to assist the user in finding relevant literature, i.e. by guiding the user. This guidance is based on user input and on the content of the data store established by the Semantic ETL process, and is employed in the current prototype. First analyses of user logs suggest the successful goal-oriented guidance of users to relevant literature. However, more usage data needs to be collected and analysed systematically before we can make statements whether the user is guided as quickly as possible. Also, user surveys are necessary to evaluate whether users have the impression that the application understands them similarly to a human librarian. Those evaluations are future work.
3. *Situation-aware*: The guiding agent component provides the logic to assess the situation of the user and adapts the guidance strategy accordingly. For example, if the user provides a general search term with too many search results, the application suggests sensible specializations. On the other hand, if the search terms are too specific to find any research result, the application suggests related terms.

10 http://jquerymobile.com/. Accessed on 29 December 2014.
11 http://knockoutjs.com/. Accessed on 29 December 2014.
12 https://github.com/ericdrowell/KineticJS/. Accessed on 29 December 2014.

4. *Intuitive*: First experiences with the prototype suggest that users are able to use the application without training or studying a user manual. However, systematic user surveys will be needed to evaluate this aspect.
5. *Device-independent*: The current prototype implementation is usable on most state-of-the-art devices and platforms, in particular Nexus 10 (Android 4.2.2 Tablet), Samsung Galaxy S3 (Android 4.1.2 Smartphone), iPad4 (iOS 6.1.3 Tablet), iPad3 (iOS 5.1.1 Tablet) and iPhone 4 (iOS 6.1 Smartphone).
6. *Good performance*: The current prototype implementation exhibits a response time below one second for common use cases.

Related work

Question answering

Ferrucci et al. (2010) give an overview of IBM's DeepQA Project and Watson, which is a Question Answering (QA) application which defeated human champions in the American TV quiz show Jeopardy. Due to the real-time requirements, particular attention is given to an architecture allowing for high performance. Watson uses numerous data sources including, for example, the YAGO ontology. Similar to our approach of semantic ETL, the data sources are pre-processed and loaded into the system in an offline process to allow for high-performance online access. While the goals and capabilities of Watson are far beyond the ones described here, we regard this as a confirmation of our Semantic ETL approach.

Search result clustering

The topic described in this paper is related to search result clustering. Because we exploit metadata, the initial task of "discovering subject of objects" (Carpineto, Osiński, Romano and Weiss 2009, 5) is a much more straightforward process, however, visualization is challenging in both disciplines. In search-result clustering, a hierarchical "folder layout" is usually employed (Carpineto et al. 2009, 16), while other, graphically sophisticated alternatives usually suffer usability problems (Carpineto et al. 2009, 18). Instead, with the topic wheel, we developed a novel approach of displaying search-result clusters with a high usability.

ETL component

Many media stock projects describe an ETL component, including those which employ a pure Semantic Web technology stack, because "in practice, many data sources still use their own schema and reference vocabularies which haven't been mapped to each other" (Mäkelä, Hyvönen and Ruotsalo 2012, 87). For example, Schreiber et al. (2008, 244) describe a considerable effort in the "harvesting, enrichment and alignment process of collection metadata and vocabularies", which takes about "1–3 weeks to include a new [media] collection" (page 248). This time is comparable with the integration effort of the Semantic ETL process, too.

Query expansion

We currently do not employ a classic query expansion mechanism, even though others like (Ruotsalo 2012) reported very good experiences in comparable problem domains. However, with the Guiding Agent, we have a similar mechanism that modifies queries, e.g. to refine a certain search request. In contrast to the classic query expansion, our approach is based on heuristics operating on result sets. Admittedly, we see some potential in query expansion in our future work.

Adaptive guides

According to Brusilovsky (2001) the landscape of adaptive guides and adaptive recommendation systems can be divided into closed-web and open-web systems. Our application is a closed-web system, it displays only content which is directly linked by authority files and library information systems such as HeBiS.[13]

The Guiding Agent makes suggestions, similar to Letizia (Liebermann 1995) and SiteIF (Stefani & Strapparava 1999). SiteIF is a closed-web and Letizia an open-web recommendation system. Letizia estimates the value of a certain link for the searching user and recommends them to the user. The recommendations are preference ordered and computed regarding the persistence of interest phenomenon (Liebermann 1995) and can even react on serendipitous connections, which is a major goal in browsing-driven behavior. Letizia uses information retrieval as well as information filtering. Both systems do not ask the user for keywords of interest, but create a user model based on the visited pages. Unlike them, the Guiding

13 http://www.hebis.de/eng/englisch_index.php. Accessed on 29 December 2014.

Agent does not employ user models, because the combination of search-oriented and browsing-oriented systems implies that the user provides the Guiding Agent with a keyword of interest, the search term. The recommendations are then made based on the structure provided by the authority files. However we see potential in user modelling in our future work.

Semantic visualization

As mentioned, Collins (Collins, Carpendale and Penn 2009) has major influence on our work, with the difference that Collins's DocuBurst visualizes the complete content of a document enabling the user to compare large amounts of text at once. DocuBurst uses WordNet (Fellbaum 1998), a lexical database, to match synonyms in a text and to detect their relationships. It visualizes structure and counts of word occurrences in a document using a sunburst diagram, which displays hierarchy and quantity distribution in circular arcs. In contrast to DocuBurst, the topic wheel described in this paper is an interactor – therefore usability weights more than utility. It limits the displayed information and appears differently in landscape and portrait modes as well as on different device classes like smartphones and tablets.

Conclusions and future work

Releasing linked open data (LOD) is currently very much in the spirit of the age. While this paradigm allows developers to incorporate world knowledge on an as yet unprecedented scale into their applications, building complex knowledge-based systems is still a challenging task.

In pursuit of recreating the utility and usability provided by a human librarian, we introduce the Mediaplatform application for situation-aware, semantically guided literature research. The application helps users to find and retrieve books, assists them by understanding their needs, and provides recommendations. The application is intuitive and shows a good performance across various different devices and platforms.

We showed that a number of different data sources and formats are to be considered. We also showed how to tackle format-specific issues and data consolidation challenges with a Semantic ETL process.

The storage structures so created are the foundation of the Guiding Agent component, which intelligently composes query results and suggestions with the help of various heuristics. Results are displayed by a HTML5 client with an innovative, rotatable topic wheel.

Early evaluations indicate that we are on the right track. The storage can cope with the metadata of about 15 million publications and first algorithms guide users to relevant literature with the help of the automatically composed topic wheel. Early user tests also show that the application can be used easily, on most state-of-the-art devices and platforms, with a good performance.

With the research and development described in this paper, we did a first important step in establishing core concepts and creating a powerful and sustainable architecture of the Mediaplatform. The prototype implementation is a proof-of-concept.

We plan to extend the functionality of components and introduce new ones. We see potential in pre-processing the user input with methods of Natural Language Processing (NLP). Thereby, entities like book titles or authors could be identified. This could then be used to conduct a query expansion, as described by Ruotsalo (2012), e.g. to find terms across different languages.

In a continuous process, we will enrich our data stores with new data sets extending the knowledge-driven guidance, as well as we will adjust the underlying heuristics. Employing a persistent user-model, as described in (Roes, Stash, Wang and Aroyo 2009), could also significantly improve the guidance mechanisms.

We will continue to constantly conduct feedback loops and usability tests with selected users, as well as we plan to systematically evaluate their expectations, experiences, and usage patterns.

We aim at transforming the research prototype towards a commercial product within the next years.

Acknowledgements

Our work is funded by the LOEWE initiative of the German state of Hesse under contract number HA 321/12-11. Cooperating partners are the University and State Library Darmstadt as customer as well as Software AG, media transfer AG, nterra GmbH and the House of IT.

References

Berners-Lee, Tim. 2009. “Linked data.” http://www.w3.org/DesignIssues/LinkedData.html. Accessed on 27 December 2014.

Bowker, Geoffrey C. and Susan Leigh Star. 1999. *Sorting Things Out: Classification and its Consequences*. Cambridge: MIT Press.

Brusilovsky, Peter. 2001. “Adaptive Hypermedia” *User Modeling and User-Adapted Interaction* 11(1-2): 87–110. doi:10.1023/A:1011143116306. Accessed on 29 December 2014.

Carpineto, Claudio, Stanisław Osiński, Giovanni Romano and Dawid Weiss. 2009. “A Survey of Web Clustering Engines” *ACM Computing Surveys* 41(3). doi:10.1145/1541880.1541884. Accessed on 29 December 2014.

Collins, Christopher, Sheelagh Carpendale and Gerald Penn. 2009. “DocuBurst: Visualizing Document Content Using Language Structure” *Computer Graphics Forum* 28(3): 1039–1046.

Deuschel, Tilman and Rita Vas. 2012. “Das Hörspielbrett: Produktion und Feldtest eines nutzer-zentrierten, interaktiven Hörspiels für Kinder im Alter von 8–11 Jahren” (master’s thesis, Hochschule Darmstadt).

Fellbaum, Christianne, ed. 1998. *WordNet: An Electronic Lexical Database*. Cambridge, Mass.: MIT Press.

Ferrucci, David, Eric Brown, Jennifer Chu-Carroll, James Fan, David Gondek, Aditya A. Kalyanpur, Adam Lally, J. William Murdock, Eric Nyberg, John Prager, Nico Schlaefer and Chris Welty. 2010. “Building Watson: An Overview of the DeepQA Project” *AI Magazine* 31(3): 59–79. http://www.aaai.org/ojs/index.php/aimagazine/article/view/2303/2165. Accessed on 29 December 2014.

Florins, Murielle and Jean Vanderdonckt. 2004. “Graceful Degradation of User Interfaces as a Design Method for Multiplatform Systems.” In *IUI ‘04 Proceedings of the 9th International Conference on Intelligent User Interfaces*, edited by John Riedl, Anthony Jameson, Daniel Billsus and Tessa Lau, 140–147. doi:10.1145/964442.964469. Accessed on 29 December 2014.

Golbeck, Jennifer, Gilberto Fragoso, Frank Hartel, Jim, Hendler, Jim Oberthaler asnd Bijan Parsia. 2003. “The National Cancer Institute’s Thesaurus and Ontology” *Web Semantics: Science, Services and Agents on The World Wide Web* 1(1): 75–80. doi:10.1016/j.websem.2003.07.007. Accessed on 27 December 2014.

Heuss, Timm. 2013. “Lessons Learned (and Questions Raised) from an Interdisciplinary Machine Translation Approach.” Position paper for the W3C Workshop on the Open Data on the Web, 23– 24 April 2013, Google Campus, Shoreditch, London. http://www.w3.org/2013/04/odw/odw13_submission_18.pdf. Accessed on 27 December 2014.

Liebermann, Henry. 1995. “Letizia: An Agent that Assists Web Browsing.” In *IJCAI’95 Proceedings of the 14th International Joint Conference on Artificial Intelligence*, 1:924–929. San Francisco: Kaufmann.

Mäkelä, Eetu, Eero Hyvönen and Tuukka Ruotsalo. 2012. “How to Deal with Massively Hetero-geneous Cultural Heritage Data – Lessons Learned in CultureSampo” *Semantic Web* 3(1): 85–109. doi:10.3233/SW-2012-0049. Accessed on 29 December 2014.

Nicolau, Hugo and Joaquim Jorge. 2012. “Touch typing using thumbs: understanding the effect of mobility and hand posture.” In *CHI ‘12 Proceedings of the SIGCHI Conference on Human*

Factors in Computing Systems, edited by Joseph A. Konstan, Ed H. Chi and Kristina Höök, 2683–2686. doi:10.1145/2207676.2208661. Accessed on 29 December 2014.

Roes, Ivo, Natalia Stash, Yiwan Wang and Laura Aroyo. 2009. "A Personalized Walk through the Museum: the CHIP Interactive Tour Guide." In *CHI '09 Extended Abstracts on Human Factors in Computing Systems*, 3317–3322. doi:10.1145/1520340.1520479. Accessed on 29 December 2014.

Ruotsalo, Tuukka. 2012. "Domain Specific Data Retrieval on the Semantic Web." In *The Semantic Web: Research and Applications: 9th Extended Semantic Web Conference, ESWC 2012, Heraklion, Crete, Greece, May 2012: Proceedings*, ed. by Elena Simperl, Philipp Cimiano, Axel Polleres, Oscar Corcho and Valentina Presutti, 422–436. Berlin: Springer. http://www.springer.com/computer/information+systems+and+applications/book/978-3-642-30283-1. Accessed on 29 December 2014.

Schreiber, Guus, Alia Amin, Lora Aroyo, Mark van Assem, Victor de Boer, Lynda Hardman, Michael Hildebrand, Borys Omelayenko, Jacco von Osenbruggen, Anna Tordai, Jan Wielemaker, Bob Wielinga. 2008. "Semantic Annotation and Search of Cultural-heritage Collections: The MultimediaN E-Culture Demonstrator" *Web Semantics: Science, Services and Agents on the World Wide Web* 6(4): 243–249. doi:10.1016/j.websem.2008.08.001. Accessed on 29 December 2014.

Stefani, Anna and Carlo Strapparava. 1999. "Exploiting NLP Techniques to Build User Model for Websites: The Use of WordNet in SiteIF." In *Proceedings of Second Workshop on Adaptive Systems and User Modeling on the World Wide Web, Toronto and Banff, Canada. Computer Science Report 99-07*, 95–100. Eindhoven: Eindhoven University of Technology.

Suchanek, Fabian, Gjergji Kasneci and Gerhard Weikum. 2007. "YAGO: a core of semantic knowledge." In *Proceedings of the 16th international conference on World Wide Web (WWW '07)*, 697–706. New York: ACM. doi:10.1145/1242572.1242667. Accessed on 27 December 2014.

Niklas Lindström and Martin Malmsten

6 Building Interfaces on a Networked Graph

Abstract: The National Library of Sweden, the Swedish Cultural Heritage Board and the Swedish National Archive have held a number of workshops with the purpose of both exposing linked data and creating interfaces built on top of multiple datasets from the participating organizations and others such as DBpedia.[1]

Having the ability to work with data from multiple stakeholders does, however, create great expectations when it comes to creating interfaces with a cohesive user experience. Historically, doing such a thing would have involved aggregating the data to one single database, which goes against the underlying principles of the architecture of the web.[2] However, linked-data technologies have evolved enough to provide the means of creating such interfaces by directly interacting with the live datasets, be they local or remote.[3]

The release of SPARQL 1.1[4] has proved a game changer in this area. Specifically, it is now possible to create federated queries across multiple datasets in a standardized and vendor-independent way.

In other words, SPARQL-enabled parts of the web of data can now be queried in real-time, furthering the vision of linked data, turning the web into a database.

On these workshops we have created a new authority view for Libris based on these technologies, drawing information from multiple sources to create a view that is more in the context of the user than in the context of the source material. This also allows for a more natural partition of responsibility regarding data. For example, influencedBy-relationships would be hard to maintain in the national catalogue, but are a natural part of Wikipedia. In the other hand, a complete bibliography and list of authors is the responsibility of the national library. Using SPARQL, a query such as "books by authors influenced by Strindberg" is easily answered providing the user with extended information that would otherwise have been impossible or costly to maintain by a single party.

This quite simple query can of course be solved by other means, but one of the points of SPARQL is that it queries the data itself, you do not have to expose a specific API for each type of query. Queries can also easily become arbitrarily complex.

1 http://dbpedia.org/. Accessed on 30 December 2014.

2 http://www.w3.org/TR/webarch/. Accessed on 29 December 2014.

3 http://www.w3.org/DesignIssues/LinkedData.html. Accessed on 29 December 2014.

4 http://www.w3.org/TR/sparql11-overview/. Accessed on 29 December 2014.

The obvious risk to this approach is inherent in the distribution of data and server infrastructure. However, since the approach mirrors that of the larger web itself, by being an actual part of it, these problems are well-known and solutions such as caching and fault-tolerance are ubiquitous today.

Keywords: Linked data, SPARQL, Federated query, Usability

Background: Islands of data

Cultural institutions today, indeed most public institutions and many companies alike, are in need of managing immense amounts of data. In order to utilize, consolidate and share this data, current practices leave a lot of room for improvement. Numerous idiomatic descriptions, sometimes haphazardly constructed and in dire need of revision, clutter the workspace of most practitioners.

And copies of such data abound, commonly modified at the site of the data consumer, thus in the process deviating from, and ultimately being disconnected from, their sources.

Linked data

> The Semantic Web isn't just about putting data on the web. It is about making links, so that a person or machine can explore the web of data. With linked data, when you have some of it, you can find other, related, data (Berners-Lee 2006).

At the National Library of Sweden, we strive to tackle this situation by applying linked-data practices in earnest. We find it crucial to work with various external data sources. The lowest hanging fruit in this field is DBpedia. It represents descriptions in Wikipedia, and enables linking to well-known phenomena, such as famous authors, etc. It also contains a huge amount of user-provided information, ranging from dates, descriptions and depictions to categorizations and named relations to other things in the dataset, such as influence.

Exposing linked data from multiple, heterogeneous datasets from multiple stakeholders, including generalized data services such as DBpedia, is of course a grand challenge. The stacks of technology that exist today promise much, but it is hard to determine what principles they will work with, and in what ways they will allow the experts to retain influence over expressions in detail, and the means of coordination.

It is necessary to create palpable applications out of these datasets, and to engage experts in creating, linking and filtering the connections that can be made. We need real, decentralized and distributed linked data, used in real scenarios.

Getting together

During 2013, we, the National Library of Sweden, along with the Swedish Cultural Heritage Board and the Swedish National Archive held a number of workshops with a dual purpose. One aspect was to expose our respective datasets as linked data, or improve on existing publishing of such data. The other, interwoven with the first, was to create interfaces built on top of these linked datasets, and along with that combine other datasets, especially DBpedia.

The target for the workshops concerning exposure of data was threefold: (1) expose a local dataset as LOD, (2) set up a SPARQL 1.1 server and (3) implement a protocol for listening to changes within the dataset (e.g. Atom, RSS, OAI-PMH).

While the workshops varied substantially in details, the basic cycle of work was the same. We focused on repeatedly performing these steps:

1. Gather data.
2. Define use case.
3. Build interface.
4. Use data.

Integration in practice

Doing this work would historically have involved aggregating the data in one single database. However, linked data technologies have evolved enough to provide the means of creating applications and interfaces by directly interacting with the live datasets, regardless of them being local or remote. Thus we only need to build upon the architecture of the web itself, using tools working directly with the web standards.

The release of SPARQL 1.1 has proved a game changer in this area. Specifically, it is now possible to create federated queries across multiple datasets in a standardized and vendor-independent way.[5] In other words, SPARQL-enabled parts of the web of data can now be queried in real time, furthering the vision of linked data, turning the web into a database.

5 http://www.w3.org/TR/sparql11-federated-query/. Accessed on 30 December 2014.

In these workshops we created a new authority view for LIBRIS based on the technologies mentioned above, drawing information from multiple sources to create a view that is more in the context of the user than in the context of the source material. This also allows for a more natural partition of responsibility regarding data. For example, "influencedBy" relationships would be hard to maintain in the national catalogue, but are a natural part of Wikipedia. In the other hand, a complete bibliography and list of authors is the responsibility of the national library. Using SPARQL, a query such as "books by authors influenced by Strindberg" is easily answered providing the user with extended information that would otherwise have been impossible or costly to maintain by a single party.

It is important to distinguish adding data from remote sources from actually using data from the same. Simply collecting triples from servers that have the same DBpedia URI is trivial and lets you decorate an interface with more information. However, to be able to say that you actually use remote data you have to draw conclusions based on it and create an understanding from the union of the datasets. Fortunately, SPARQL in general and SPARQL 1.1 was created with this in mind.

Following are screenshots from the running application (Figures 6.1, 6.2, p. 89). They depict views of authors, where details include formal label (from LIBRIS), a descriptive text and thumbnail image (from DBpedia), a list of works (LIBRIS), and then a list of other authors, that exists in LIBRIS, which the current author have been influenced by.

A simple code base

We chose a set of simple tools for building an application. A primary goal was to express the domain-specific data gathering as SPARQL queries, and to render that in a web application with a fairly small amount of code. The web application itself, written in Python, built upon the Flask Requests[6] and RDFLib[7] Python packages,[8] is less than 200 lines of code (or around 520 words), excluding templates and queries.

6 http://flask.pocoo.org/. Accessed on 30 December 2014.

7 http://docs.python-requests.org/en/latest/. Accessed on 30 December 2014.

8 https://github.com/RDFLib. Accessed on 30 December 2014.

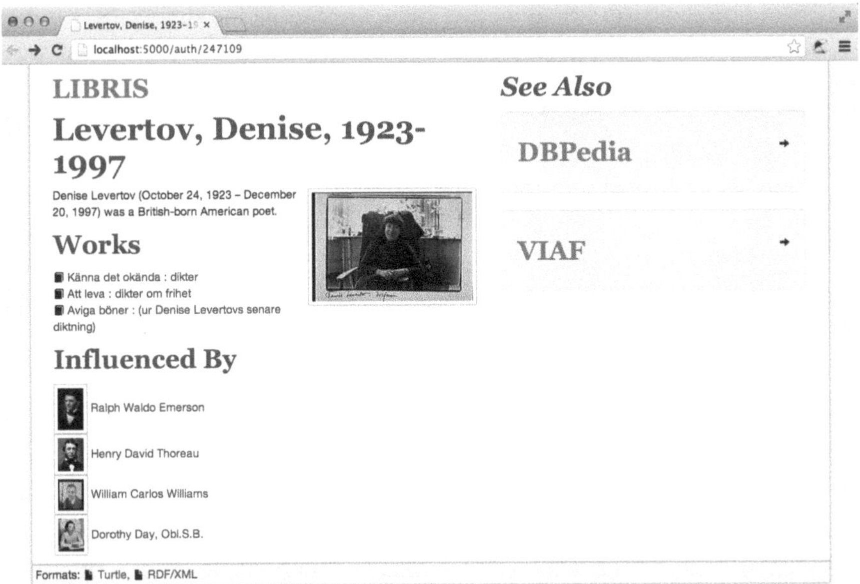

Figure 6.1: A mix of data from LIBRIS and DBpedia

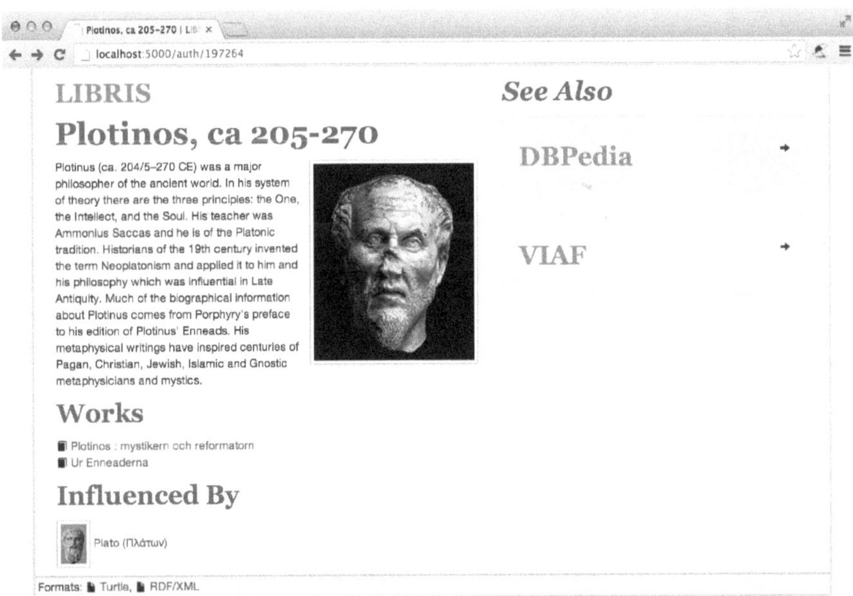

Figure 6.2: Almost every influence chain leads to a classical philosopher...

Below are some excerpts from that code, illustrating the simplicity of using standards to handle the HTTP protocol and RDF data format in a regular web application:

```
from rdflib import Graph
from requests import post
from flask import render_template
#
def view(uri):
...
query = render_template("queries/auth.rq", this=uri)
response = post(ENDPOINT, data={'query': query})
graph = Graph().parse(data=response.content)
return render_template('auth.html',
**dict(view_context, this=graph.resource(uri)))
```

One SPARQL query is used to create the influence listing depicted in the previous section, running over a live combination of data from LIBRIS and DBpedia. It matches an "owl:sameAs" relation in LIBRIS pointing to a DBpedia identifier, then matches persons listed as "dbpowl:influencedBy" in DBpedia, and finally matches those to authors described in LIBRIS. Relevant parts are shown below.

```
PREFIX foaf: <http://xmlns.com/foaf/0.1/>
PREFIX owl: <http://www.w3.org/2002/07/owl#>
PREFIX dbpowl: <http://dbpedia.org/ontology/>
#
CONSTRUCT {
...
} WHERE {
...
} UNION {
<http://libris.kb.se/resource/auth/247109>
owl:sameAs ?same .
SERVICE <http://dbpedia.org/sparql> {
...
OPTIONAL {
?same dbpowl:influencedBy ?same_influence .
...
}
}
OPTIONAL {
FILTER(BOUND(?influence))
```

```
  ?influence owl:sameAs ?same_influence .
  }
  }
...
```

Usability comes from usage

The ability to work with data from multiple stakeholders must be combined with expectations of interfaces with a cohesive user experience. The process of turning an idea into a working application is always a revealing experience. What seems simple on paper can often turn into interesting twists and turns. For instance, ensuring consistent use of identifiers, describing enough details around the kinds of connection between a person and its creations, as well as distinguishing features of such works, requires well-established principles and consistency. That is paramount in order to cross the gap between dataset boundaries. This is a cultural and intellectual challenge, and intrinsically a social activity. At the centre of this are the activities around data creation, and more crucially, data usage.

Linked data + UX = Actually useful data

While an important piece of the strategy, Tim Berner-Lee's five star model[9] is not quite enough here. You need to decide on tangible usage, with clearly defined actors, behaviors and intents, and goals for their activities. And you need to invite people into your data as much as possible. SPARQL is an enabling technology for this – a very powerful one. Still, recognition is key. In order to combine descriptions, you must understand their parts. Also, in order for data to be fit for re-use, you have to eat your own dog food (or drink your own champagne, depending on how you rate your code)! While data is mostly valuable when shared, if you do not use it yourselves, you have no ground for sustainable dialogue around it.

9 http://5stardata.info/. Accessed on 30 December 2014.

Data usage, understanding and quality

Some key aspects affect the practical capabilities of using data:

- Form– how is the data described? As a basis for this, we need shared and used vocabularies. That constitutes a common ground of simple understanding, and can draw on the collective experience and consensus of experts in their own fields. The sharing of such vocabularies is an intrinsic part of the linked-data strategy. This is not enough in itself though, since the value is often lost when properties fall into disuse. You must ensure that the terms are applicable in real usage.
- Identity– what is the thing described? Being able to precisely define a phenomenon, be it physical or intellectual, is in theory an endless philosophical challenge, with hard questions around temporality and mereology. Nevertheless, a practical stance and effective, applied practice has shown that any central ontological enigma can be basically ignored, as long as you stay within the realm of common sense. Still, it requires a fair amount of discipline, and above all as much consistency as possible across domains. This must be acknowledged and evident to those producing data. It is not enough to jot down items of observation, you have to have a clear idea of what the subject is – the resource being described. It does not have to represent "objective reality" as long as it is readily explainable. Lots of possible integration is lost when triples are used as raw record data instead of actual resource descriptions.

There must be room for flexibility as well. There is a difference between dirty data (e.g. denormalized data with crude string values, disparate properties, etc.) and broken data (incorrect identifiers, undefined properties or logical contradictions). A certain amount of noise is not only tolerable, but a rather natural effect of specific and somewhat different intents in different activities, sectors and organizations. There are still ways to coordinate these on the vocabulary level. Although beyond the scope of this paper, we'd like to say that fairly often, it can be as simple as using the "sub-property of" link relation defined in RDF Schema for that to happen. A very fundamental thing to realize is that different people in different contexts utilize various levels of generalization when conceptualizing a phenomenon. Some focus on the enduring aspect of a physical exemplar (or a set of unmodified bytes in a digital pattern), whilst others are interested in the commonality of sets of such exemplars (exemplified by such notions as "expression" or "work").

Again, as long as this can be indicated in the description of the resource (or at least in information about the dataset wherein the description resides), by some means of vocabulary, multiple levels can work together in practice, by means of giving them precise identities and well-defined links between them.

Challenges

The obvious risk to this approach is inherent in the distribution of data and server infrastructure. However, since the approach mirrors that of the larger web itself, by being an actual part of it, these problems are well-known and solutions such as caching and fault-tolerance are ubiquitous today.

Network limitations – cache is king

Principally, using federated SPARQL lets us opt out of the syndication problem. Setting up a proxy cache in front of external endpoints is a simple way of persisting snapshots of results. Due to the sole basis of HTTP, such an operation changes nothing in the application layer (apart from the chosen service URLs, which are configurable, atomic and enumerable).

To speed up work with our application, we have used nginx[10] as a caching reverse HTTP proxy configured to ignore cache control headers, and also to cache POST requests. In configuration code, this simply becomes:

```
proxy_cache_methods GET POST;
proxy_cache_key "$request_uri|$request_body";
proxy_ignore_headers Expires Cache-Control;
!
location /dbpedia/sparql {
proxy_pass http://dbpedia.org/sparql;
}
!
location /dewey/sparql {
proxy_pass http://dewey.info/sparql.php;
}
```

This captures the outgoing calls to e.g. DBpedia, and the query time for a specific view can be reduced to a negligible amount, after an initial invocation. We can do this kind of aggressive caching since we know that data is intermittently updated, and we accept to make our own decision when to clear the cache and refresh. This ensures that we can have a working system utilizing remote data to enrich its views, even if the remote endpoint is unstable. The exact decision procedure for cache duration can of course be further refined and improved, possibly even involving experts deciding if a refresh is to be trusted.

10 http://nginx.org/. Accessed on 30 December 2014.

This is comparable to a data-service lookup and storage of results, with the difference here that the architecture still behaves as if complete, live remote integration is active. And therefore, we can expire caches when the remote services are updated, or coming back online after an outage, etc. with no compromise at all to the application layer, which is built on the principles of a distributed knowledge base.

While caching solves the performance and some of the stability problem if an endpoint is often unreachable and/or unstable for any cause, it may simply not be a good candidate for integration into your interface. In the end it comes down to trust or possibility of an agreement with the dataset provider.

The main point is that this should not change the model.

Cache vs Aggregate

It is important to realize that while stability issues are inherent in this approach, they can be handled. This uncertainty often leads to creation of big aggregates of data since "the web cannot be trusted". We feel strongly that if there is a problem with "the internet" it should be solved within said internet, rather than trying to create aggregates, essentially local copies.

The difference between a cache and an aggregate is the level of transparency. A cache is invisible, while an aggregate is often a conflation of a cache and workspace. Aggregates also comes with certain problems when it comes to curation. Should you curate your data in the aggregate or at the source? Our position is that curation in the aggregate is waste.

Indexes as sophisticated caches

There are limits to what graph stores with SPARQL endpoints are capable of today. Certain kinds of free-text search with faceted filtering and sorting are currently tricky to solve in general. And there are better instruments for that today, such as the Lucene-based[11] search platforms Solr and Elasticsearch.[12] These tools are advanced indexes over text in tree-structured data. By treating them as sophisticated caches upon snapshots (tree-shaped subgraphs) of interest, you can go beyond what the standards allow for today, without breaking the distributed architecture we describe here. That is, as long as you use them solely for optimi-

11 http://lucene.apache.org/. Accessed on 30 December 2014.
12 http://www.elasticsearch.org/. Accessed on 30 December 2014.

zation, and not live containers of data, the linked data practices for decentralized data will work just fine.

Conclusion: Future federations of knowledge

With this, we have shown a means of combining local datasets and building interactive experiences, in order to achieve a generally usable quality. We have done this by resting on distributed principles, and by striving for as much interlinking across datasets as possible.

One of the basic points of SPARQL is that it queries the data directly as-is. The example queries in this paper can of course be solved by other means. But you don't have to expose a specific API for each type of query. SPARQL allows for arbitrary excursions into your datasets. And queries can be used to answer quite complex questions, spanning several systems across the web.

The best way for putting linked data into practice is to build user interfaces and work out how the descriptions combine and can yield new connections. This effectively uncovers hidden problems like missing data, mismatched assumptions or inconsistencies and contradictions.

Securing the stability of these kinds of federated networks of data can also be done without formally breaking the distributed principle. We have shown that simply applying caching in the HTTP layer works just as well here as it does for the web at large. Even specialized indexes can be treated as simply advanced caches. We can thus ensure an important point: that the sources of data are the best places for curating that data. That is where the experts reside. By using distributed principles, you can assemble data from any local experts you choose to trust. Without relocating anything.

These possibilities and practices are still rather nascent, and there is lots to be done for this federated data architecture to become well-known and continue to mature. It is important to show how simple integration can be, and to build tools upon this infrastructure, to ensure that small players with local data can publish their own data, and leverage others', without the constraints they have today, using legacy tools and expensive pipelines. Putting the power of data usage, curation and consolidation into the hands of domain experts in all kinds of settings is the only way the web of data can evolve properly, without being mired by large aggregation services who regularly displace the ownership of quality data. The responsibility for the quality of data must be in the hands of domain experts, at the same time these experts must realize the importance of usability and connectedness.

There are also several other steps which can evolve from this stable core. We need additional data, created by the subsequent users (sometimes thought of as "end users"). To achieve this, systems need to enable them to enrich the existing descriptions, based on their specific needs. It can be as simple as providing a means for suggesting missing details. Such data can, again transparently, be incorporated into the inner layers of a system.

One way of doing so is to treat user-contributed data as suggestions of patches, which can be incorporated at the source and become part of the dataset. Another way, based on the federated linked data pattern, is to give users ability to create additional facts in their own local systems, enriching the description of subjects of other datasets. This in effect constitutes user datasets, which can be integrated by the means described in this paper, as long as this data is published as LOD.

That is, transparently, without compromising the integrity of the original data. Because datasets can be dynamically added when creating a view from multiple sources. The user can thus herself choose what to trust when such a view is generated.

Such a functionality would provide tangible results to users from contributing information of value to them, including links to external resources, encouraging further activity in this space.

In conclusion, our message is this: technology for federated access to linked data, and means of building applications upon that, is mature enough for real usage, via proper user interfaces, to take place. In so doing, the data will be at the center of activity, and will thus undergo continuous evaluation and improvement. This can happen at the source, and as a net effect will benefit everybody who is consuming it.

Acknowledgements

We are grateful for the cooperation and participation by our fellow Swedish cultural heritage institutions for participating in the workshops, and for taking a progressive stance in a world of legacy structures. We'd like to thank our colleagues at the National Library of Sweden for working with us in driving this technology and strategy forward, and for diligently handling all the ideas we throw around. And of course, to the linked data practitioners at large, especially the Wikipedia and DBpedia communities.

References

Berners-Lee, Tim. 2009. “Linked data.” http://www.w3.org/DesignIssues/LinkedData.html. Accessed on 27 December 2014.

Natasha Simons, Arve Solland and Jan Hettenhausen

7 Griffith Research Hub

Connecting an Entire University's Research Enterprise

Abstract: Universities are operating in a knowledge environment characterized by competition, collaboration, a diversification of research outputs and rapid technological change. Thus the use of linked data is rapidly gaining momentum, typically for educational resources, with research as a subset of this content. The Griffith Research Hub is focused specifically on exposing linked data for research. It provides a publicly accessible, single comprehensive view of Griffith University's research output and activities, including research publications, projects, datasets, centres, researchers and their collaborators. The Hub serves an ambitiously wide audience including higher-degree research students, researchers, industry and the media. Built in-house on open-source semantic-web technologies, the Hub draws data automatically from multiple enterprise systems and includes an edit interface for manual correction and enrichment of data. The Hub is the product of a partnership between Griffith University and the Australian National Data Service. Benefits of the Hub include powerful yet simple search and browse tools; generation of substantial web traffic; linked data that allows users to seamlessly discover related information in other services and databases (including Trove at the National Library of Australia); visualization features and the development of a shared ontology to describe research activities.

Keywords: Semantic Web Technologies; Research; Linked Data; Data Visualization; Collaboration; Research Datasets; Libraries.

Introduction

Universities and research institutions are operating in a knowledge environment characterized by rapid technological change, global competition and collaboration, a significant increase in digital information and a broadening of research outputs beyond publications to include data as a first-class output of research. A global community of scholars is emerging that is connected and collaborative but also competitive in nature. Increasingly, private and government funding bodies are seeking a better return on their investments in research, and consequently institutions need to take note and provide related evidence. There is an environment of global competitiveness between research institutions for funding, for staff and for students. Indeed, the research impact of a university can make a significant contribution to university league table measures (O'Brien 2010). As new technologies continue to develop rapidly, institutions need to seize the opportunity by utilizing these in their research endeavours and showcasing their researchers and their achievements. University linked data, particularly when made publicly available, offers advantages in this competitive environment as it facilitates resource discovery, integration of data sources, visualization and deep faceted searching across multiple data sources regardless of their format.

The growing number of publication and conference presentations on the use of linked-data in a university environment show that this approach is gaining momentum. D'Aguin (2011) suggests that linkeddata "... is now widely recognised as a critical step forward for the Higher Education sector in the UK (and worldwide)". Reflecting on rapid changes in the education sector which are transforming universities from a physical place into a virtual organization, d'Aguin (2014) suggests this is creating a perfect environment for linked data to flourish. The Open University in the United Kingdom was the first university to expose its data as linked data (d'Aguin 2011). This was achieved through the LUCERO (Linking University Content for Education and Research Online) project which has been the topic of various conference papers and presentations. Drivers for the project included enabling transparency and re-use of the data, both internally and externally to the institution; reduction of costs, and enabling new types of applications to be developed while making existing ones more feasible. Kessler and Kauppinen (2012) discuss linked data at the University of Münster, suggesting the expansion of research materials to include not only papers but data, models and software which need to be preserved in order to be reproducible. They argue that "the different scientific resources, be they publications, datasets, method or tools should be annotated, interlinked and openly shared in order to make science more transparent and reproducible..." (2012, 1).

Transparency and reproducibility of research, along with a need to capture the diversity of research outputs, are clear motivators for linked-data projects that expose university research. However, many of the examples of university linked data in literature examine projects that encompass university-wide data, in particular learning and teaching data. Research data is generally included in such projects but as one part of a wider scope. Additionally, some of these projects have not included development of a discovery interface for users, instead focusing on data exposure through machine-to-machine queries. The Griffith Research Hub[1] project differs in that its scope was confined to research data: publications, grants, datasets, research groups and public researcher profiles. The Hub also

1 Griffith Research Hub, http://research-hub.griffith.edu.au. Accessed on 18 March 2015.

differs in that it began with external funding to develop a metadata store for data relating to research datasets and, through additional rounds of internal funding, now includes more data sources and exposes its linked data through a public interface designed for discovery of the University's researchers and their research materials.

Overview

The Research Hub is described on the home page as "a rich and informative guide to the University's expertise in a comprehensive array of academic fields". It provides a single, comprehensive view of Griffith University's research activities and outputs. Built in-house on semantic-web technologies and officially launched in June 2012, the Hub has drawn significant web traffic to the University. It serves as a showcase for Griffith research and contains profile pages of Griffith researchers and their associated groups and research centres, projects and grants, publications, research data collections, and a small number of services. The Hub can be found through the home page URL or via a Google search. It serves an ambitiously wide audience including international researchers looking for collaborators, research students looking for supervisors, industry looking for consultants, and journalists looking for expert sources. The Hub can be browsed or searched by keyword, discipline, researcher name or field of expertise.

Figure 7.1 (p. 101) shows the top portion of the Research Hub profile page for Associate Professor Rodney Stewart. The page contains his photograph, position title, school affiliation and contact details at the top. The page is then divided using tabs. The Overview tab includes research centre membership, a short biographical statement, and research areas. The Publications tab lists the publications authored by the researcher, divided into publication types and then ordered by year. There is a Projects tab that lists grants, a Collections tab to display research data collections that Associate Professor Stewart is associated with and a tab that lists his supervisory experience, specifically the theses produced by higher-degree research students whom he has supervised. There is a Background tab that includes a wide variety of information from tertiary qualifications through to awards and internships. The links tab includes links to other websites relevant to the researcher.

The profile page also includes two colourful and interactive graphs. The top graph is a multi-layer ring visualization of a researcher's publications by fields of research. The fields of research are drawn from the Australian and New Zealand

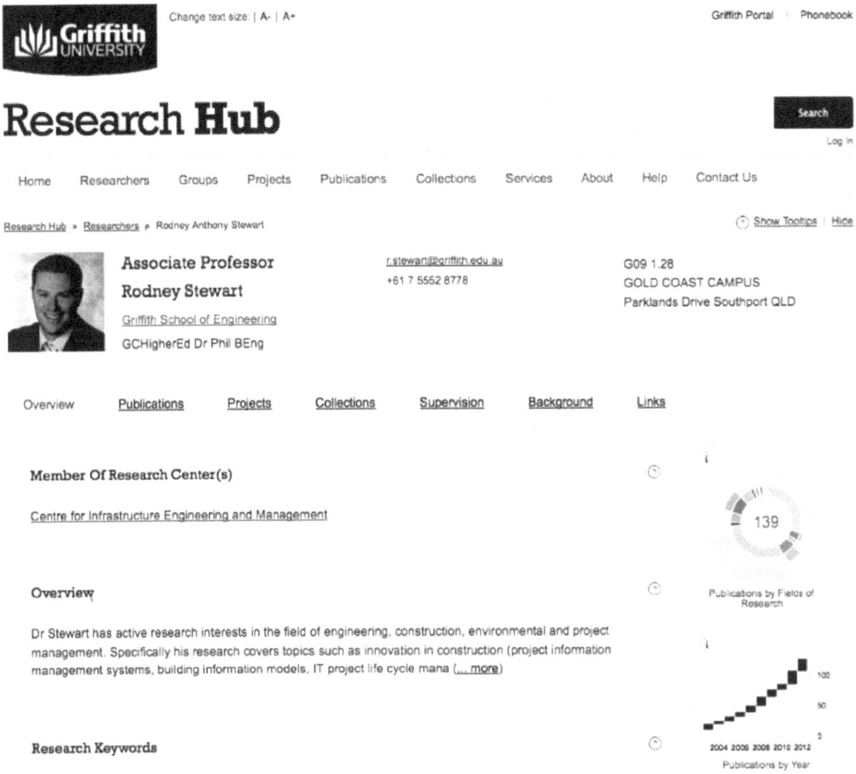

Figure 7.1: Research Hub profile page

Standard Research Classification (ANZSRC) Field of Research codes[2] that are routinely assigned to publications eligible for Australian government reporting purposes. When users hover their mouse on each slice of the ring, a pop-up provides information about the field of research area. Each slice can be clicked on to open the list of publications for that field of research area. The second graph is a researcher's publications by year with the red representing new additions for each year. Users can hover their mouse over the red slice to see a pop-up of the number of additional publications. Clicking on the slice will open a list of the additional publications. The two graphs are unique to each researcher in the Hub. We discuss their development in the section on linked-data visualization.

While all publications and projects associated with Griffith are discoverable through the Hub, not all Griffith researchers have a profile page in the Hub. Those that do have met certain criteria relating to number of publications and the eli-

2 ANZSRC, http://www.arc.gov.au/applicants/codes.htm. Accessed on 18 March 2015.

gibility of those publications for government reporting purposes. Inclusion is calculated automatically based on publications that have been entered into the Griffith publications portal. The driver behind the selective process is to ensure that researcher profile pages are rich in information quantity and quality.

The Hub contains 1,000+ researcher profile pages; 60+ groups; 5,000+ projects; 56,000+ publications; 50+ research data collections and 10+ services. These figures are updated after a nightly ingest of new and updated data. The most up-to-date statistics can be found by clicking on each of the tabs listed on the Hub home page.

The Hub was developed using open-source tools to extract and combine information from a variety of enterprise data sources. Data is linked, aggregated and presented in an accessible semantic web system. A Resource Description Framework (RDF)[3] triple store is used to model complex relationships between entities. The linked-data model enables users to seamlessly browse from a researcher's profile to an article, a project, a dataset and so on. The Hub project included the development of an ontology to describe research activity that is now widely used outside the project (discussed in detail later in this article). Hub data is also shared with other systems and services, for example the National Library of Australia's Trove[4] and the Australian National Data Service's Research Data Australia portal.

The achievements of the Hub as a technological innovation filling the need for a single comprehensive view of the university's research output has been recognised in two prestigious awards: the VALA Award 2012 and a Commendation of Merit in the Stanford Prize for Innovation in Research Libraries 2013.

The Research Hub project

The Australian National Data Service (ANDS)[5] provided funding for the initial development of the Research Hub, with Griffith subsequently contributing additional funding. As a response to the rapidly increasing size and complexity of research data, ANDS was established as a government-funded organization to lead the creation of a cohesive Australian collection of research resources and a richer data environment. Wolski and Richardson outline the various drivers for the initial Hub project, noting that "undoubtedly one of the largest deterrents is

---

3 W3C Semantic Web, Resource Description Framework, http://www.w3.org/RDF/ . Accessed on 18 March 2015.

4 NLA, Trove, http://trove.nla.gov.au/. Accessed on 18 March 2015.

5 ANDS, Australian National Data Service, http://ands.org.au/. Accessed on 18 March 2015.

the effort required of researchers not only to locate their data, but also to format it for sharing" (2010, 3).

The initial funding for the Hub was provided through the ANDS Metadata Stores Program.[6] The goal of this Program has been to ensure that metadata relating to research data collections is well managed so that it can be harvested and exposed to search engines, researchers and research administrators. A key objective is to enable metadata harvesting by ANDS for inclusion in Research Data Australia (RDA),[7] the flagship service of ANDS that enables discovery of Australian research data collections. RDA is a growing service that contains more than 85, 000 research datasets or collections of research materials contributed by over 80 Australian research institutions.

The purpose of the ANDS Metadata Stores Program is to support research institutions to develop an enterprise solution for the discovery and re-use of their research data collections. The Program follows on from previous government funding for institutions to identify and capture data about the university's research datasets. The aim of creating an institutional metadata store is to ensure metadata records that describe datasets are well managed and exposed for sharing with researchers and research administrators as well as other services, such as the ANDS Research Data Australia portal, via metadata harvesting and indexing by search engines.

In the context of the Program, a Metadata Store is a central system at an institution that can house metadata records that describe research data collections in addition to associated researchers, research groups, services and so forth. In this model, research data itself is not stored but a link is provided to the system that stores the data files. Relevant metadata is automatically drawn from various systems across a university and compiled in a single system for exposure to search engines and harvesters.

The initial funding from ANDS enabled Griffith University to develop a "Metadata Exchange Hub". For this purpose, we selected VIVO,[8] a loosely coupled open-source semantic-web application originally developed in 2004 at Cornell University. According to the VIVO website,[9] the application "enables the discovery of research and scholarship across disciplines at that institution and beyond". At

6 ANDS, Metadata Stores Solutions, http://www.ands.org.au/guides/metadata-stores-solutions.html. Accessed on 18 March 2015.

7 ANDS, Research Data Australia, http://researchdata.ands.org.au/. Accessed on 18 March 2015.

8 VIVO, http://vivo.sourceforge.net/. Accessed on 18 March 2015.

9 VIVO Frequently Asked Questions http://www.vivoweb.org/about/faq/about-project. Accessed on 15 March 2015.

the time, there was no requirement for the metadata store to have a public view but we saw the potential for the linked-data metadata store to be developed into a comprehensive researcher-profile system that could publicly showcase Griffith researchers and their outputs. This required additional internal funding. The team developed a project proposal and won the support of the Office for Research. Internal funding was provided that more than matched the funding from ANDS and so began a fruitful partnership between the Griffith Office for Research (business owner of the Hub), the Division of Information Services (service provider of the Hub) and ANDS. Key to the success of this partnership was the demonstrator model (provided through Cornell), a shared vision, and a spirit of innovation and experimentation.

How the Hub works

Griffith University, like all universities and many organizations, has multiple systems and data sources spread across departments. These information silos make it difficult for researchers to find the information they need, because they are not linked to other databases or systems. Because of this, researchers have to go to each individual database to search for the required information. Additionally, information in each separate database is generally limited in providing connections to information in other databases. As a result, some data is duplicated between the systems and there are inconsistencies. Researchers are also frustrated because they are asked to enter the same data in multiple systems. Griffith's many information silos include a publications repository, a research data repository, a personnel database, and a research administration database. The Hub addresses such a challenge by drawing data automatically from databases within the University and linking that information – using URIs wherever possible – for discovery and re-use. Additionally, the Hub describes the relationships between the objects or entities in the databases. This semantic-web model enables richer data mining, improves Google indexing and allows users to use linked data to discover a wealth and depth of information not previously possible.

The Hub has an automatic nightly ingest of data from multiple enterprise databases including:

- Griffith Research Administration Database: this database contains information about grants, research centres and publications;
- The Griffith Metadirectory: this system is a source of public human resource information such as names and contact details of researchers;

- The Griffith Research Data Repository: this repository contains metadata records that describe research data collections and, in many cases, the data itself;
- The Griffith Theses Repository: this repository contains metadata records about theses produced by Griffith higher-degree research students and their supervisors.

The Griffith Division of Information Services (incorporating both the Library and Information Communication Technology Services) maintains the repositories, in addition to maintaining a publications repository, Griffith Research Online (GRO).[10] While the Hub does not draw information directly from GRO, it does include metadata descriptions of publications with a web link to the GRO record that allows users of the Hub to discover further information and download the publication (if available). Similarly, the Hub draws metadata about research data collections for the data repository and provides a link back to the full metadata record and data files (where available) in the data repository. This linked-data model allows users of the Hub to discover this information in new ways by providing additional context and discovery points. Further, because the Research Hub is built on a semantic-web platform using RDF, it is well indexed by Google and therefore draws more web traffic to the institution compared with the publications repository.

The Hub also periodically ingests information about people and groups from the National Library of Australia's (NLA) Trove discovery service. This information takes the form of unique identifiers assigned to Griffith researchers by the National Library of Australia that resolve back to a unique page in Trove. Currently the NLA identifiers for researchers are stored but not displayed in the user interface of the Research Hub. They may be exposed in the future along with other researcher identifiers such as the Open Researcher and Contributor ID (ORCID)[11] in order to provide the user with additional linked data discovery points.

In addition to being well indexed by Google, a metadata harvesting end point is provided by the Research Hub. This is used by the National Library of Australia to harvest information about researchers and research groups into Trove. It is also used by ANDS to harvest metadata records about research data into Research Data Australia. The records harvested from Griffith by the NLA are displayed in the Trove People and Organisations zone and contain a link back to a more extensive record in Research Data Australia. The records in RDA contain links back to the Research Hub. Figure 7.2 (p. 106) illustrates the data model for the Research Hub.

10 Griffith Research Online, http://www98.griffith.edu.au/dspace/. Accessed on 18 March 2015.
11 ORCID, http://orcid.org/. Accessed on 18 March 2015.

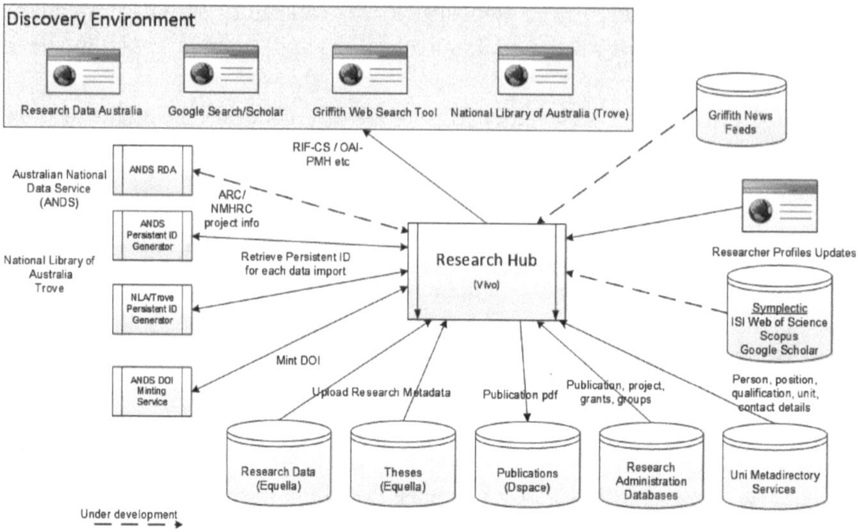

Figure 7.2: Data model for the Research Hub

Technical architecture

Griffith selected VIVO as the software to use for the "Metadata Exchange Hub" project for a variety of reasons. Some of the most important features were:
- strong MVC (Model View Controller) separation in architecture;
- storing the data in a graph database, aka a "triple store";
- rich administration interface to allow ontology editing, data management and presentation configuration for the system;
- easy and direct way to display semantic data, in an accessible way from the triple store through well-developed template languages.

VIVO offered strong support for all of these elements, and had in addition a very active developer community which enabled us to get instant help, and access to resources and developers that had been part of the origins of the VIVO software development.

Being early adopters of any software has its implications, both positive and negative. The international VIVO development community provided an environment in which we were able to actively participate, share ideas, and to a certain extent steer the development of certain functionality elements into the direction we saw as best practice and most fitting for our requirements. However, it also meant that we were exposed to early bugs, lack of documentation, unfinished functionality and so forth. This created some additional work on our side and at times we had to move away from the streamlined VIVO functionality path to create local functionality that would suit the emerging requirements for our Research Hub.

During the project phase, the requirements for the Research Hub changed as we encountered new situations, e.g. the Hub exposed data that had not previously been displayed in a publicly accessible, easy-to-find interface. As this data was not always correct or comprehensive, and generated complaints from researchers profiled in the Hub, we decided to build an edit interface to enable researchers to login, correct and augment information on their profile page. The changing system requirements also meant that the standard functionality of the VIVO software had to be re-addressed or extended to support our new or changed requirements. However as the project progressed, we found that the core functionality of VIVO was very strong and we could quite easily plug our in-house developed modifications into it and extend it to create the product we needed.

Using library linked data

An increasing number of universities are making the decision to expose their linked data to the public. Library linked data, as a specific type of data in a university environment, offers many advantages. In 2011, Stanford University linked-data workshop participants "... shared a vision of Linked Data as a disruptor technology with the potential to move libraries and other information providers beyond the restrictions of MARC based metadata as well as the restrictions of many variant forms of metadata generated for the wide variety of genres in use in scholarly communication" (Keller et al. 2011, 5). Many libraries have exposed their catalogues as linked data, such as the American Library of Congress and the German National Library of Economics. However, library linked data can included broader sources than the catalogue, such as institutional publication and data repositories. This library data, when coupled with additional external data sources, has great potential for creating a more powerful search and discovery experience for users.

The linked nature of the data presented in the user interface of the Research Hub is definitely one of its best features. Linked data enables users to browse from a researcher's profile to an article, and then to the profiles of the co-authors of the article, to the projects related to any of those co-authors, and so on. It offers a rich, natural, accessible and connected view of all the research work undertaken at Griffith University and exposes it to the world. It also showcases the cross-disciplinary and highly collaborative nature of research at Griffith University.

All individual entities in the Hub are allocated their own publicly accessible landing page in which the information about the individual is displayed via a rich, semantically enabled HTML interface. These HTML landing pages can contain specific attributes such as RDFa or microdata to specifically describe the content displayed. This is extremely beneficial when a machine, such as a search-engine crawler, reads the page, as it specifically describes what the content is and how things are related. As an example, the landing page for a publication will contain information in the mark-up, invisible to a normal user, that this is an Information Resource, who the authors are and so on. When this information is made specifically available to search engines, it gives the content a good chance of a high ranking in search results. In fact, after turning on this additional metadata in the landing page, a significantly higher ranking for landing pages in the Hub was achieved in a very short time.

In addition to providing HTML landing pages for entities in the system, the Research Hub provides multiple Open Archives Initiative Protocol for Metadata Harvesting (OAI-PMH)-compliant feeds[12] to specifically enable harvest of specific metadata by external systems. To setup our OAI feeds we have used the very flexible MOAI[13] system. MOAI is an open access server platform for institutional repositories. It is set up to query the Hub for specific metadata, combine the queried records into different sets and publish them via the OAI-PMH.

Some of the external systems harvesting from the OAI feeds setup in the Research Hub include Research Data Australia, National Library of Australia's Trove, Research Papers in Economics (RePEc)[14] and Open Language Archives Community (OLAC).[15] In addition, the Griffith site-wide search uses a comprehensive OAI feed from the Research Hub to populate its search engine with metadata about the research activities contained in the Hub.

These OAI feeds provide an effective way of automating the exchange between commonly used systems and portals. For example, the Trove service from National Library of Australia harvests the OAI feed from the Research Hub to get metadata related to Griffith researchers exposed in this feed. The OAI feed also exposes the Trove identifier for the researchers where one has been previously assigned. This helps the Trove service identify any researchers who might not already have a

12 OAI-PMH, http://www.openarchives.org/pmh/. Accessed on 18 March 2015.
13 MOAI, http://moai.infrae.com/. Accessed on 18 March 2015.
14 Research Papers in Economics, http://repec.org/. Accessed on 18 March 2015.
15 Open Language Archives Community, http://www.language-archives.org/. Accessed on 18 March 2015.

Trove identifier and supports processes to disambiguate records about different researchers with the same name. If needed, Trove can generate a new identifier for a researcher and this Trove identifier can then again be automatically harvested back into the Research Hub, leading to richer data about the individual and easier disambiguation in external systems.

Byrne and Goddard (2010) argue that librarians are well positioned to understand and implement linked data because of their skills in metadata creation, search and ontology development. It is worth noting that the Research Hub Project was managed within the Griffith University Division of Information Services (INS). The Pro-Vice-Chancellor (INS) was a Hub Board member and the Project Manager was a librarian, bringing leadership and expertise from the library sector into the project.

Streamlining data import

The Research Hub relies on nightly automated data ingests from a variety of systems, as illustrated in Figure 7.3 (p. 110). Data ingest involves extracting and loading data from external source systems into VIVO. The data in the source systems are all in various formats and structures. Therefore, we needed to streamline this process so that the data going into the Hub's triple store is all in a uniform format. The incoming data also needed to be mapped into VIVO's core ontologies, our locally developed ontologies and external ontologies for describing research and library data. This way, the data can be available for consumption via a rich, semantic HTML page, raw RDF XML data, or via OAI-PMH feeds.

To facilitate our ingests, we decided to use an ETL (Extract Transform Load) tool called Jedox[16] that can extract data from a multitude of different data sources and formats. Data sources could be SQL databases, flat files, web services or other types. During the ingest process, the data from the various sources are loaded into the Jedox tool, where they are transformed, or mapped, to the desired output format using the available ontologies and vocabularies to describe the data. This way, if we are getting information about people from different systems, in different formats, we can have the output of the data from the different data sources rendered in a uniform format, controlled by chosen ontologies.

One of the great benefits of using a triple store with ontologies describing the data is how easy it is to extend the data model with new attributes or properties.

16 Jedox, http://www.jedox.com. The Jedox ETL tool is available as open source at http://sourceforge.net/projects/palo/. Accessed on 21 January 2015.

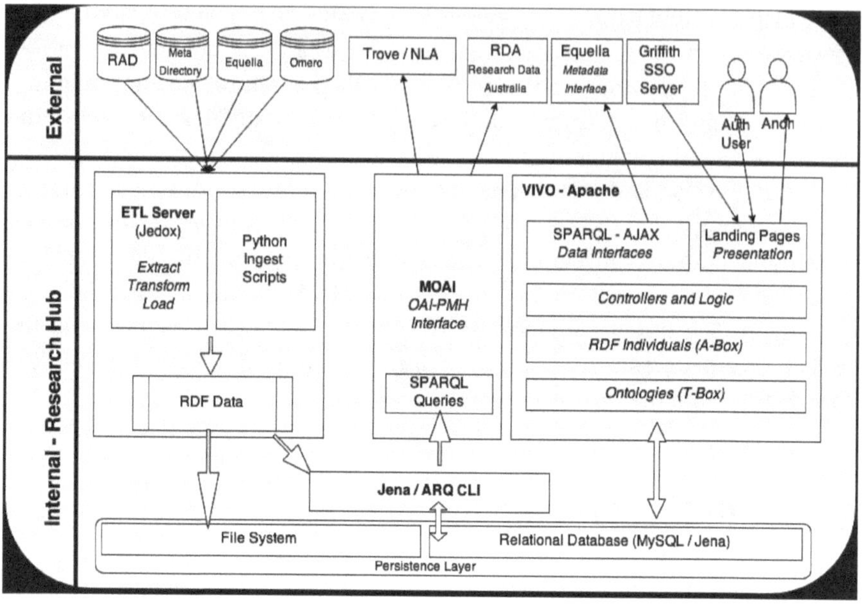

Figure 7.3: Research Hub architecture diagram

A simple example is different identifiers generated by different systems. For example, a publication will have a unique identifier in the Research Hub, but could also have other identifiers, such as a Digital Object Identifier or an International Standard Book Number. Ontologies including these properties can then be added to the triple store, thereby creating a rich variety of fields that accurately identifies the object in external systems.

When the data has been transformed/mapped into the output format, it is ready to load into the Hub's triple store. We developed a differential model script for ingest as we could not accurately determine the timestamp of change for all data elements in external systems. The script ensures that only changed or new data is loaded into the Hub every night. This model reduces the server load on ingest and better and more accurately timestamps the changed data. The script takes the output data from the ETL tool, compares it with the last ingest output, and only loads new or changed data into the triple store with a correct last-modified timestamp.

Developing an ontology for research activities

To comprehensively describe the research activities at Griffith University and put them into an Australian context, a new ontology called the ANDS-VITRO ontology was developed.[17] The ANDS-VITRO ontology extends the VIVO ontology to cover research datasets, as well as the vocabulary and structure required by ANDS based on the Registry Interchange Format – Collections and Services (RIF-CS)[18] schema used for contributing records to Research Data Australia. The development of this ontology was initiated and led by Griffith University in collaboration with the University of Melbourne and Queensland University of Technology.

The ANDS-VITRO ontology describes and maps information about research activities into formally defined and commonly used concepts in the education sector, for example, the Australian Bureau of Statistics' hierarchical vocabulary for ANZSRC codes that are routinely assigned to research publications.[19] The relationships between these concepts are detailed and can be used to perform additional reasoning among the concepts in that domain. For example, searches of the Hub can be extended with broader and narrower scope based on the linking hierarchical fields of research definitions.

The ANDS-VITRO ontology received significant uptake and broad community support after it was developed because it created a much needed shared vocabulary and taxonomy that closely models the domain of research activity in Australia. The ontology has been widely adopted by institutions with completely different software stacks but the same underlying approach towards a shared definition of Australian research activities.

The community using the ANDS-VIVO ontology has marshalled several requirement changes and updates to the requirements and future additions of the ANDS RIF-CS Schema, the Research Data Australia Service and linkage with Trove. In addition, extensions and enhancements developed in the ANDS-VIVO ontology have been adopted by the VIVO ontology maintainers, and are now part of the shared vocabulary of VIVO's widespread high-impact international research community, for example, the International Researcher Network.[20]

---

17 ANDS-VITRO Ontology, https://github.com/anzsrco/ands. Accessed on 18 March 2015.

18 Registry Interchange Format – Collections and Services Schema, http://www.ands.org.au/resource/rif-cs.html. Accessed on 18 March 2015.

19 ANZSRC ontology, https://github.com/anzsrco/anzsrco

20 International Researcher Network, http://nrn.cns.iu.edu/. Accessed on 18 March 2015.

Linked-data visualization

An intriguing challenge of having a large amount of linked and formally described data available is to present it to the user in a useful and meaningful way. While textual information definitely serves an important purpose in the Hub by providing users with comprehensive data, data visualization allows users to quickly tackle this large amount of data, gain an understanding and hopefully engage them in further discovery. The nature of the linked data in the Hub has provided an ideal basis for developing visualizations to enhance the users' experience of using the Hub. Given the diverse audience for the Hub, ranging from other researchers to members of the media and the general public, we were particularly interested in using visualization combined with interactivity to give users an intuitive tool to discover and explore our researchers' research interests and publications.

At present we have developed two different graphs for this purpose, visualizing the research areas and research "velocity" of each researcher. We felt in particular that a graphical representation of research areas would be useful to expert and non-expert users as this information is notoriously hard to gauge from publication lists and project titles. Short descriptions and free text keywords may provide some insight but are only available where researchers have added them. Furthermore, the possibility of using them for further search and discovery is limited.

In the development of a research area graph we made use of the fact that government reporting of research output in Australia mandates that publications be associated with research areas from the ANZSRC Field of Research code vocabulary. This puts us in the unique position of being able to query research areas as well as the broader research categories for these areas in our Hub RDF data. To represent this hierarchical data in an intuitively understandable way we developed our research area chart based on a multi-layer ring chart (see Figure 7.4, p. 113). The inner ring of this chart represents broader research areas, derived using the Field of Research ontology, while the outer ring represents the research areas directly gathered from publication data. The arc width of the slices on both rings is a proportional representation of the number of publications in this area. To reflect that publications can be more or less focused on one area, the radii of the outer slices are not fixed but instead determined by a metric of Field of Research code diversity of these publications.

For the visualization of publication velocity we have chosen a stacked bar-chart graph, showing for each year how many publications in total a researcher has published up until this year and how many have been published in that year. An example of this graph can be found in Figure 7.5 (p. 113). The graph replaces

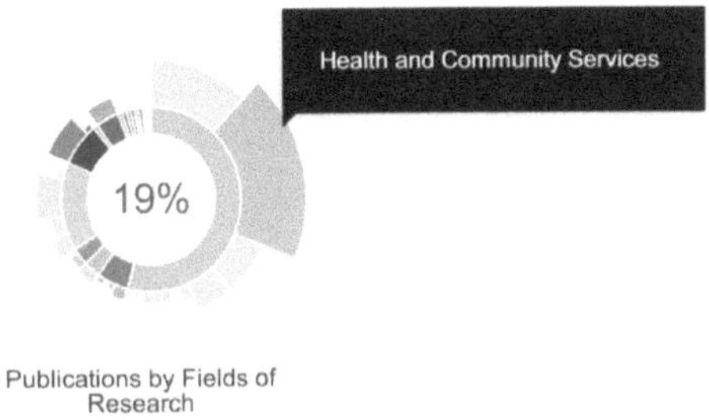

Figure 7.4: Chart visualizing the research areas of a researcher. Hovering the mouse over a field will bring up a tooltip showing the title of the respective slice. Clicking on a slice will trigger a search for matching publications for that researcher.

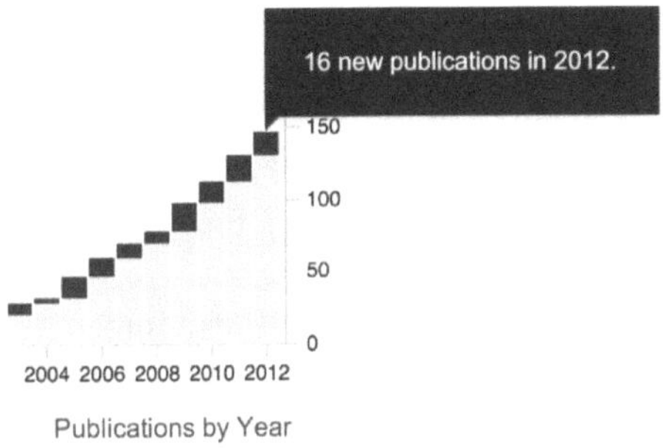

Figure 7.5: Chart illustrating the cumulative research output of a researcher for the previous ten years. Hovering the mouse over an element will show the number of publications for that year. Clicking any segment of a bar will trigger a search for publications made in that year.

a Sparkline-based visualization of publication velocity, as we found that it more intuitively represents the research output as measured by number of publications.

In both visualizations all graph elements are clickable, triggering a search for the publications they represent. In the search, the user can then select additional facets to narrow down their search further or select publications to view their metadata and download the associated document, if available.

Following user feedback both visualizations will in the future be added to the pages of research groups, institutes and similar organisational units. For these entities they will show the data of all affiliated researchers with the search feature adapted accordingly. A production release of this update is currently pending.

Challenges of source data

In NISO's *Information Standards Quarterly* topical issue on "Linked Data for Libraries, Archives and Museums", Stevenson (2012) discusses the challenges of aggregating data from multiple sources. She reflects that data sources are invariably inconsistent, subject to change without notice and error prone. Stevenson suggests that for aggregators working with data from external sources, the lack of control over these sources is one of the major issues with linked data. Indeed, publicly exposing the error-prone and inconsistent information from source databases has been the major challenge for the Research Hub project.

The Hub draws information from multiple enterprise systems and although only publicly available information from these systems is selected for display, exposing the information initially raised significant problems with data quality. For example, a researcher's qualification dates may have been recorded incorrectly in the personnel database or the name of a project funded by a research grant may have changed and not been updated in the grants database. In addition, our source databases are subject to updates and system upgrades that may affect ingest of data from these systems into the Hub.

Stevenson suggests that broadly speaking there are two alternative approaches to working with problematic data in external source databases: address inconsistencies in the transformation process or address problems at the source. The Research Hub solution differs slightly. Wherever possible, changes to information displayed in the Research Hub are corrected in the original enterprise system that feeds such information to the Hub. The corrections then automatically flow through to the Hub with the automated nightly ingest. However, in some cases correction of the data in the source enterprise system is not possible. Therefore an edit interface was created in the Hub to enable researchers to log in and correct certain information that can't be corrected in the source, such as qualification dates. The edit interface also includes the ability to augment information to compensate for the absence of such information in source databases. For example, a researcher can add a biographical statement, upload a photograph and create research area keywords.

Implementing a self-edit model in which designated information can be corrected or augmented has the added benefit of giving researchers some control over the information that is displayed on their profile page. This is an aspect that researchers really appreciate. As researchers are usually time-poor, we also built in permissions that allow them to nominate someone, such as an administrative assistant, to edit their profile page on their behalf. It is not a requirement of the Hub that researchers update their profile pages but it is certainly beneficial in order to provide an optimal profile to the high volume of web traffic the Hub attracts.

It is important to note that the Research Hub has only replaced two of the source systems feeding the Hub. Other source systems will remain in place with local control, as they serve broader purposes. For example, the University's grants database has a critical government reporting function that includes private information not exposed through the Hub. Therefore our hybrid model of correcting data in the source system where possible and otherwise using the self-edit interface to correct the information needs to continue into the future.

Project challenges

Reflecting on their experiences developing linked data infrastructure and applications at the University of Münster, Kessler and Kauppinen (2012) suggest that beyond the technical infrastructure it was necessary to foster change in the mindset of the university research community. This was also a challenge for the Research Hub team: to communicate with the university research community about the new system and ways in which they could engage with it. The key to this was the involvement of the Office for Research, the university's provider of research services, research quality development, and support. The Office for Research was the business owner of the Hub throughout the project, while the project was implemented by INS. This provided leadership and authority from both the Office for Research and INS, which assisted our communication with researchers about the Hub. The Division of Information Services provided the project team of software developers, technical analysts and a project manager. The Office for Research and the Division of Information Services worked in partnership toward a shared vision of a researcher profile system that could be seen in the examples set by other VIVO users, including Cornell University[21] and the University of Melbourne.[22]

As early implementers of VIVO, the Hub project team had to overcome technical issues and deal with complexity. Reaching agreement with various data owners to access information drawn from enterprise systems was also a hurdle. Another major challenge was the aggregation and public exposure of information from multiple enterprise systems. As discussed, data quality and comprehensive-

---

21 VIVO: Research & Expertise across Cornell http://vivo.cornell.edu/. Accessed on 18 March 2015.

22 University of Melbourne: Find an Expert http://findanexpert.unimelb.edu.au/. Accessed on 18 March 2015.

ness became an issue immediately after the Hub was launched. At the time, Griffith researchers checked their Hub profiles for the first time and this resulted in a stream of requests for assistance in correcting or providing additional information. The project team responded to this by shifting from developing the system to maintaining it by responding to researchers' requests. Occasionally this meant changes to the VIVO code or the ontology. After the initial few months, the requests slowed and the team continued with further system development.

The nature of project work is that it has a definite end point, usually when all project deliverables have been met or when funding has been spent. It is quite challenging to develop a model of sustainability that ensures the output of the project, in our case the Research Hub, continues to be maintained and supported. Because the Hub was built based on a strong internal partnership, and because it has been so successful in achieving its aims, Griffith University will continue to not only maintain the Hub but to further develop it. The sustainability model includes the Division of Information Services as the business owner with technical support provided by the eResearch Services and IT enterprise systems and infrastructure teams. A range of documentation has been developed to assist technical and administrative support staff. Contextual help and FAQs are incorporated into the Hub to assist researchers in finding information and editing their profile pages and a "contact us" form can be used for help from the Hub technical team. At a broader level, Griffith is represented on the VIVO Board and sends representatives to VIVO conferences, both national and international. Hub technical team members are active participants in the VIVO community and Griffith has made its customization of VIVO available as open source code[23] and ontology development freely available.

Lessons learned during the course of the project can be summarized as:

1. Develop a strategy to win internal support;
2. Cultivate partnerships with stakeholders and funders;
3. Negotiate access to data from different enterprise systems;
4. Develop a plan to address the inevitable data quality issues;
5. Nurture the project team;
6. Demonstrate value to the institution and funding bodies;
7. Embed the product in the institution;
8. Articulate success through statistics and updates;
9. Build a sustainability model;
10. Develop a roadmap for future development.

23 Griffith University's VIVO customizations, https://github.com/gu-eresearch/VIVO. Accessed on 18 March 2015.

In the future, the scope of the Hub may broaden to include profile pages and related content for all Griffith academic staff. It will also be important to maintain the back end of the system, for example VIVO upgrades and patches, and to expand the front end to include more visualizations and so on. There are plans to include metrics and altmetrics in the Hub at the article level and to integrate the Hub with Symplectic Elements.[24] It is also likely that the number and type of databases feeding the Hub will be expanded and this will present an opportunity to expose more linked data to users. Given the success of the Research Hub to date, we are confident that the Hub will continue to develop well into the future.

Conclusion

The Research Hub exposes linked data relating to research using sources within the library as well as external to it, including linked data exchanged with other institutions such as the National Library. Built on open-source, semantic-web technologies with initial funding from ANDS, it has been highly successful in driving web traffic to the Griffith University, thereby increasing the public visibility of its researchers and their outputs. The Hub demonstrates what can be achieved when an institution seizes the opportunity and commits itself to developing a linked-data discovery service.

References

Byrne, Gillian and Lisa Goddard. 2010. "The Strongest Link: Libraries and Linked Data." *D-Lib Magazine* 16. doi:10.1045/november2010-byrne. Accessed on 18 March 2015.

d'Aguin, Mathieu. 2011. "Building the Open University's Web of Linked Data" [Slideshare presentation]. http://www.slideshare.net/mdaquin/building-the-open-universitys-web-of-linked-data. Accessed on 18 March 2015.

d'Aguin, Mathieu. 2012. "Linked Data for Open and Distance Learning." Report prepared for the Commonwealth of Learning. 2nd ed. http://www.col.org/PublicationDocuments/LinkedDataForODL.pdf. Accessed on 18 March 2015.

Keller, Michael A. et al. 2011. "Report on the Stanford Linked Data Workshop." http://www.clir.org/pubs/reports/pub152/LinkedDataWorkshop.pdf . Accessed on 18 March 2015.

Kessler, Carsten and Tomi Kauppinen. 2012. "Linked Open Data University of Münster – Infrastructure and Applications." Presentation at Extended Semantic Web Conference 2012 (ESWC2012), Greece. http://kauppinen.net/tomi/lodum-eswc-2012.pdf. Accessed on 18 March 2015.

24 Symplectic Elements, http://www.symplectic.co.uk. Accessed on 18 March 2015.

O'Brien, Linda. 2010. "The Changing Scholarly Information Landscape: Reinventing Information Services to Increase Research Impact." Presentation at ELPUB2010 – Conference on Electronic Publishing, Helsinki. http://hdl.handle.net/10072/32050. Accessed on 18 March 2015.

Stevenson, Jane. 2012. "Linking Lives: Creating An End-User Interface Using Linked Data." *Information Standards Quarterly* 24:14–23. doi:10.3789/isqv24n2-3.2012.03. Accessed on 18 March 2015.

Wolski, Malcolm and Joanna Richardson. 2010. "Moving Researchers Across The eResearch Chasm." *Ariadne* 65:1–10. http://www.ariadne.ac.uk/issue65/wolski-richardson/. Accessed on 18 March 2015.

Contributors

Emmanuelle Bermès, Centre George Pompidou, Paris, France. manue.fig@gmail.com

Michael Buckland, University of California, Berkeley, United States. buckland@ischool.berkeley.edu

Tilman Deuschel, Darmstadt University of Applied Sciences, Darmstadt, Germany. tilman.deuschel@h-da.de

Paola Di Maio, Universal Interfaces Research Lab, Institute of Socio Technical Complex Systems. www.istcs.org

Torsten Fröhlich, Darmstadt University of Applied Sciences, Darmstadt, Germany. torsten.froehlich@h-da.de

Patrick Golden, The Emma Goldman Papers, Berkeley, United States. ptgolden@berkeley.edu

Thomas Herth, media transfer AG, Darmstadt, Germany. therth@mtg.de

Jan Hettenhausen, Griffith University, Queensland, Australia

Timm Heuss, Darmstadt University of Applied Sciences, Darmstadt, Germany. timm.heuss@h-da.de

Bernhard Humm, Darmstadt University of Applied Sciences, Darmstadt, Germany. bernhard.humm@h-da.de

Patrick Le Bœuf, Bibliothèque nationale de France, Paris, France. patrick.le-boeuf@bnf.fr

Niklas Lindström, LIBRIS, National Library of Sweden

Martin Malmsten, LIBRIS, National Library of Sweden

Oliver Mitesser, University and State Library, Darmstadt, Germany. mitesser@ulb.tu-darmstadt.de

Ryan Shaw, University of North Carolina, Chapel Hill, United States. ryanshaw@unc.edu

Natasha Simons, Griffith University, Queensland, Australia

Arve Solland, Griffith University, Queensland, Australia

Index

agile development 5
archives 21, 22, 24, 32, 48, 50, 64
autocomplete 45

Bibframe 33
bibliographic information 32, 33, 45
bibliographic metadata 60

cataloguing 36, 46
Creative Commons 32
CSS 73, 78

data model 23, 24, 26, 28, 35, 37, 46, 54
DBpedia 28, 39, 56, 59, 69, 85, 86, 87, 88, 89, 90, 93, 96
Deutsche Nationalbibliothek 56
DocuBurst 74, 81, 83
Dublin Core 21, 32

EAD 21, 32
Elasticsearch 94
encoded archival description, *see* EAD
EndNote 51
ergonomics 45
extraction, transformation, and loading, *see* Semantic ETL

five star model 91
Flask Requests 88
format transformation 70
FRBR 5, 33, 34, 36, 46

Gallica 32, 41
general systems theory 10
Geonames 59
German National Library, *see* Deutsche Nationalbibliothek

HeBiS 80
HTML 54
human computer interaction 11
hypertext markup language, *see* HTML

IFLA 33, 34, 47
International Federation of Library Associations, *see* IFLA
International Standard Book Number, *see* ISBN
ISBN 33, 44

JSON 32, 70

KineticJS 78
Knockout 78

Letizia 80, 83
linked data model 4
LOD 66, 67, 68, 69, 81, 87, 96
Lucene 77, 94

manifestation 46
MARC 21, 32, 47
Margaret Sanger Papers Project 48
Mediaplatform 66, 76, 77, 81, 82
MODS 21

name authority 50, 52
National Library of Sweden 85, 86, 87, 96

OCLC 5, 34
online public access catalogue, *see* OPAC
ontology 7, 69
OPAC 36, 46
open data 22, 31, 32, 33, 34, 35, 36, 47, 66, 68, 81, 83
OWL 69
OWLim 77

prosopography 53

RAMEAU subject indexing language 36
RDA 5
RDF 23, 24, 26, 28, 32, 33, 70, 77, 90, 92
RDFLib 88
Relation Query Language 35
resource definition framework, *see* RDF
Semantic ETL 69, 71, 72, 76, 77, 78, 79, 80, 81

semantic enrichment 70
semantic web 19, 21, 31, 32, 33, 35, 36, 47, 65, 83, 84, 86
SiteIF 80, 84
SKOS 36, 69
Solr 94
SPARQL 23, 35, 69, 85, 87, 88, 90, 91, 93, 94, 95
special collections 48, 64
state machine 73

temporal metadata 60

uniform title 34, 45
union catalogue 46
usability 46, 75, 79, 81, 82, 95

VIAF 56, 59, 65
Videomuseum 21
visualization 28, 29, 52, 55, 61, 73, 74, 75, 79

WordNet 81, 83, 84
working notes 48, 50, 51, 52, 53, 59, 61, 62, 63

YAGO ontology 69, 79

Zotero 51, 55

Kolibri 360 GmbH
Ferdinand-Jühlke-Straße 7
99095 Erfurt, Deutschland
produktsicherheit@kolibri360.de